Other Books by the Author

1. Hitting The Target In Soulwinning
2. Foundation Bible Course (16 Lessons)

THE ULTIMATE DISCIPLE

Becoming Like Christ

Dr. Bennett U. Okafor

WESTBOW
PRESS
A DIVISION OF THOMAS NELSON
& ZONDERVAN

WestBow Press books may be ordered through booksellers or by contacting:

WestBow Press
A Division of Thomas Nelson & Zondervan
1663 Liberty Drive
Bloomington, IN 47403
www.westbowpress.com
1 (866) 928-1240

ISBN: 978-1-4908-1828-3 (sc)
ISBN: 978-1-4908-1829-0 (hc)
ISBN: 978-1-4908-1827-6 (e)

Library of Congress Control Number: 2013922049

Printed in the United States of America.

WestBow Press rev. date: 04/28/2014

DEDICATION

Dedicated to:
God Almighty, our heavenly **Father**,
Jesus Christ, His Son (our Lord and Saviour), and to
the **Holy Spirit** (our great Teacher and Counsellor).

To everyone who, while awaiting the return of the
Lord, desires to fully manifest the divine nature
and character of the Lord Jesus in this life.

ACKNOWLEDGEMENTS

I acknowledge the help of God Almighty and his Son, Jesus Christ, in the writing of this book. Truly, the Holy Spirit has been my great Source and Helper.

Many thanks go to all my teachers and pastors over many years. I cannot name you all in this book, but God knows every one of you and he will surely reward you.

Great thanks to my wife, Laide, and my daughter, Oluchi, for all your love. Special thanks to Tenedee Ngito (who helped a lot in making this book a reality), Mercy Jeremiah (who typed the manuscripts) as well as to Cedric Onuh.

I do acknowledge that I might have missed out some other attributes of Christ in this book but I pray that the Holy Spirit will fill those gaps for every reader.

I also acknowledge, before God, my utter unworthiness and inadequacy in writing this important book. However, he has enabled me to write it. Thanks to God for his all-sufficient grace.

Sincerely, the writer covets the prayers of every reader. Please pray for me.

Dr Bennett U. Okafor

ENDORSEMENT

I have known and admired Dr. Bennett Okafor and his dear wife, Laide, over the years. They and their children are all practising medical doctors, and are true living examples of the Christian faith. Dr Okafor is an avid soul winner and an ordained minister of Christ. His wife is an intercessor, and they have ministry work going on in different nations.

The Book, *"The Ultimate Disciple"*, is a great contribution to the development of the Christian faith both in our nation and elsewhere, and should attract worldwide distribution because of its timeliness and relevance. These are the end-times when many who profess Christ are merely holding on to *"a form of godliness, denying the power thereof"*, and living like the rest of the world.

Dr. Okafor refocuses our gaze on the glory and character of the living Christ so we can behold Him and be transformed by the Spirit of God into His image, from one level of glory to a higher level of glory. Through this, we make our calling and election sure. This Book is eminently suitable for bringing many others into true Christian discipleship, and positively influencing our world for Jesus.

I wish you a happy reading, and pray that God will grant you a more glorious transformation into the image of His Son.

The Most Rev. Ignatius C.O. Kattey (JP)
Dean, Church of Nigeria (The Anglican Communion),
Archbishop, Province of Niger Delta &
Bishop, Diocese of Niger Delta North.

ENDORSEMENT

Dr. Bennett Okafor is well known to the Assemblies of God, Nigeria. His missionary Organization, the National Evangelism Christian Outreach (NECO) Inc., is a great friend of our Church, and we have worked together with him in different fronts.

As a Patron of their Organization and a friend of the Author, I write to highly recommend this great Book, which clearly reveals the nature and character of our Lord Jesus Christ so that we can all emulate him. By highlighting the common sins and pitfalls that tend to entrap many Christians, the author warns us to be more careful and circumspect in our walk with the Lord. Clearly, we make heaven by grace, but grace is not cheap: we must keep walking with the Lord in the strait and narrow way.

May God bless you as you read and may His Spirit enable you to make heaven with flying colours! Indeed, this Book will be a wonderful companion for you along the way.

Rev. Prof. Paul Emeka
General Superintendent,
Assemblies of God,
Nigeria.

CONTENTS

ATTRIBUTES

Chapter One

THE PURPOSE OF THIS BOOK:

THE ULTIMATE DISCIPLE

Models Needed

The Kingdom of God (and God's church today) is in dire need of more men and women whose lives will model and manifest Christ to their world: in their offices, their homes, neighbourhoods, and everywhere. We are in great need of people whose lives will clearly exemplify the character and nature of the Christ of the Bible so that the world will see and believe in him. The world has heard a lot about the Lord Jesus Christ, but they have not seen so much of him through the lives of many of those who profess him. It is only as we grow more closely into his image and stature that our testimony of him will become more believable in the world.

Christ so trained and taught his disciples that even when he had gone, they were able to represent him. Thus, the Jewish leaders "took knowledge of them that they had been with Jesus."[1] Today, the world needs to take knowledge of us, too, that we have been with Jesus.

This book is designed to help you develop a closer walk with Jesus, and to become a true disciple of Christ. A disciple is a follower, a student or pupil, a trainee or apprentice of someone else, the master. In this case, you are a student, studying to become like Christ. Thus, this book is for every follower of Christ (whether you have just known him today or you have walked with him for seventy years); it contains something, which the Holy Spirit will use to quicken your spirit in your walk with the Lord.

Transformation from Worldliness

'For by grace are ye saved through faith, and that not of yourselves, it is the gift of God, not of works, lest any man should boast.' (Eph. 2:8)

Most of us (Christians) have been in the world for years before the Lord called us to live for him. And even after our call, we still remain in the world. In the course of our interactions with the world's people, we have imbibed certain vices of the world (this is apart from the sin-nature we all inherited from the first Adam).

Our salvation from sin and sin's penalty was instantaneous through the death and resurrection of Christ, and our faith in him. But God desires not only that we be saved from our sins, but that we should be mortify (crucify) the old sin-nature that indwelt us, by the help of the Holy Spirit (Romans 8:13). He wants us to become overcomers of sin, Satan, and the world through his Holy Spirit that indwells us.

This victorious new life initiated by Christ (in us) does not come into full manifestation at once: we are not made perfect at once, but we grow in grace, we grow into perfection through the renewal of our minds. Thus, Paul said:

*And be not conformed to this world, but be ye
transformed by the renewing of your mind, that ye may
prove what is that good, and acceptable, and perfect,
will of God* (Romans 12:2).

Therefore, this book is to aid us to experience God's promise of transformation, which is his perfect will for every one of his children. He does not want us to linger on in the stages of Christian childhood, when, due to age we ought to be teachers[3]. Like butterflies from their cocoons or eagles from their aeries, he wants us to emerge and fly away from our old life of sin and worldliness into the new world of grace, power and purity which Christ has prepared for us. God wants us to grow into the very image and stature of his Son Jesus Christ, whom he has given us for a model. And as we gaze upon him with open face, God's infallible Word promises that we shall be *"changed into the same image from glory to glory, even as by the Spirit of the Lord"* (2 Corinthians 3:18).

The Ultimate Model

Unfortunately, there are many Christians with different role-models today. Some of them may include politicians, army generals, sergeants, missionaries, film stars, scientists, Nobel Peace Prize Laureates, Hollywood/Nollywood actors, musicians, human rights activists, professors, housewives, church leaders, etc. Some of these may not even be Christians at all, but, for one reason or the other, something about them challenges some of us, and we adopt them as role-models or mentors.

Some Christians do not even take the Lord Jesus as their role model. They think either he is another historical figure, or they consider him too meek or too holy or some other thing. This is often because of our ignorance of God, because we spend so much valuable time with the worldly people and their programmes, and spend little time in the things of the Lord.

Howbeit, in this book we have taken Jesus Christ as our role model, the living Lord of heaven and earth, who died and rose again from the dead; the one who defeated Satan at the cross of Calvary, and who purchased eternal salvation for all humanity, and opened for us all the gateway of heaven. There is absolutely no one like him, no one ever loved like him, did the kind of miracles he did or lived a blameless and sinless life like he did.

No one was ever as compassionate and loving as he was. None was ever as humble as Jesus, the Lord who made the heavens and the earth, and yet came to wash his disciples' feet, and to die for the sins of the people he created. Today, there is no one in the whole world that commands the respect he commands, no one is nearly so popular. He commands allegiance of billions of people, many of whom would willingly lay down their lives for him. We give him all glory and honour and adoration, and bow before his Lordship.

In this book, we present some of the distinguishing attributes of this great Lord, the Lamb of God, and the great Lion of the tribe of Judah. We will also deal with seven common sins and pitfalls that many saints often fall into, and which threaten their very salvation. By recognizing them, we can, by grace, avert or overcome them, and live triumphantly for the Lord.

As you study Christ's attributes and life, endeavour to emulate him, and your life will never be the same again. The Spirit of the Lord will transform you into the same image from glory to glory. Amen.

WORK BOOK

a) The world has heard a lot about Jesus, but has not seen so much of him through the lives of those who profess him. Discuss this statement.

b) What evidence do you personally have, to show that you have been with Jesus?

c) In what ways have we all imbibed the sinful nature of the world? In which areas are you focusing to be different?

d) How is the mind renewed? Explain how mind-renewal can transform an individual.

e) We are to be changed into the same image of Christ, "from glory to glory." Explain.

f) Who are your role models today?

g) Why should Christ be our role model par excellence?

h) Summarize the message of this chapter in your own words.

i) In life events, practise:
   • What would Jesus think?
   • What would Jesus say?
   • What would Jesus do?

Chapter Two

WE WERE FOREKNOWN AND PREDESTINED

Beloved, it is amazing and certainly thrilling to know that even before you were born, and even before the foundation of the world, God Almighty had foreknown you[4], and fore-ordained that you would be his child through Christ Jesus. Isn't this wonderful?

"According as he hath chosen us in him before the foundation of the world, that we should be holy and without blame before him in love: Having predestined us unto the adoption of children by Jesus Christ to himself, according to the good pleasure of his will" (Ephesians 1:4-5).

This is why Apostle Peter also addressed us as: *"Elect, according to the foreknowledge of God the Father, through sanctification of the Spirit, unto obedience and sprinkling of the blood of Jesus Christ"* (1 Peter 1:2).

God is awesome in counsel, his knowledge is unsearchable, and his ways are beyond our comprehension. He is the Almighty and his power is limitless; whatever he has purposed to do, nothing can stop him from bringing it to pass.

God's Unspeakable Love for Us

The second mystery revealed in Scriptures is when Christ was slain, *"The Lamb slain from the foundation of the world"* (Revelation 13:8); what this means is that God had foreknown and foreordained that Christ would die for the sins of the world, right from the foundation of the world.

What all these things mean is that God's plan for our salvation was not a hurried package. God had long ago, sometime in eternity past, planned for your salvation and deliverance from sin. And the God-head had agreed to accomplish this through the coming of Christ into the world 2000 years ago, and his subsequent death on the cross for our sins. That is, before you and I were born, God had of his own choice determined that he would himself come into the world, and die for our sins.

This is why God's love is beyond human understanding: Why should a righteous, holy and perfect God come into a world laden with iniquity, and die for his own creatures?

We may never fully understand the nature of God's love, and certainly not in this life! But all we can do is to give him glory and thanks continually for his unspeakable love, and use the rest of our lives to live for his glory and praise, forever and ever! Amen.

Predestined to Become Like Christ

Dear friend, God is yet to finish his work in your life. Although he has concluded the payment for our sins for ever and redeemed us to himself as his dear children (through the death and resurrection of Christ), he is still working in us both to will and to do of his own good pleasure (Phil 2:13). Christ Jesus defeated Satan at the cross of Calvary, and gave us victory and liberty to live as victorious sons of God. He has written our names in the book of life and has bequeathed us his blessed Holy Spirit to help us and be with us forever.

Yet, God has great plans for your life and future. He wants to grow and groom you into the very image and stature of his Son, Jesus Christ our Lord!

> For whom he did foreknow, he also did predestinate to be conformed to the image of his Son, that he might be the firstborn among many brethren. Moreover whom he did predestinate, them he also called: and whom he called, them he also justified; and whom he justified, them he also glorified (Romans 8:29-30).

God's on-going plan for your life is that you should be conformed to the image of Christ, his Son: so that Jesus Christ would be the firstborn among many brethren. This means that God's will is that you should be one of the brothers of Jesus (from the same God parenthood with him) and that you should be like Jesus yourself! You are to talk like Jesus, think his thoughts, do what Jesus would do, and be a perfect reflection of the person of Jesus on earth. We are to be his ambassadors on earth, reflecting his personality to our world. Those who never knew about Jesus would know him when they see us, and interact with us.

Before you were born again you were in the world. You were carrying the image of the world, the image and nature of the first Adam (the image of sinful humanity, corrupt according to its deceitful lusts). We all followed the multitude to do evil, until Christ found us. Now God wants to change that old image that you and I had[5].

He wants us to drop that excess baggage of sin that we carried out of Egypt. He wants to stamp on you the image of his Christ, so that you will resemble his beloved Son! He wants you to reflect the new nature of his Son who is indwelling you by the Spirit.

The New (Divine) Nature

However, what is the nature of Christ? God revealed it in the Bible, especially in the gospels and in the epistles. Christ is perfect in all things, and in all his ways: so God wants to perfect everything concerning you. Christ is sinless, blameless, without deceit, without fault. Christ's nature is beautiful beyond description. He is pure, holy, just, righteous and altogether lovely. He is true, faithful, loyal, trustworthy, and full of integrity, transparency and honour.

He is gentle, kind and peaceable. He is altogether good, the best of the best. God wants to make you like him. God's plan is to make something beautiful and glorious out of you! God wants to do this work of transforming you right now, while you are still in this world, so that he can display you before the world, before men and angels, as one of his treasured finished products. Alleluia!

It is not God's plan to hurry you off to heaven with the nature of the first Adam. Sure, he has cleansed you with the blood of his Son, forgiven you all trespasses and filled you with his Holy Spirit, but he also wants your vile nature, my vile nature – our vile natures – changed forever! This transformation is not an overnight work that God is doing in us, it is a process; day-by-day God is working a beautiful work in the lives of all his children. God wants us to understand this, and to cooperate with him and yield to him, who is the Master-sculptor and Potter, so as to achieve a perfect finish of his design. He wants to make a masterpiece out of us. Therefore, *"Yield yourselves unto God, as those that are alive from the dead, and your members as instruments of righteousness unto God"* (Romans 6:13).

Transformation: Unto A Perfect Man

No wonder, Paul urged for our transformation by the renewing of our minds through the word of God, the indwelling Holy Spirit and the work of the ministers of Christ. God wants us to grow *"...till we all come in the unity of the faith, and of the knowledge of the Son of God, unto a perfect man, unto the measure of the stature of the fullness of Christ..."* (Ephesians 4:11-13).

God's plan is far more astounding than many of us can imagine! He wants to build us up, teach us, and grow us by his Spirit, until we become fully-grown spiritual adult sons of God, standing with Christ shoulder-to-shoulder in maturity, holiness, wisdom, love, and in everything else, unto a perfect man (that is, unto the measure of the fullness of the stature of Christ); yet in perfect submission to him as our Creator, Lord, Redeemer and Saviour!

The devil thought he had things well wrapped up when he deceived Adam and took the birth-right from humanity, and killed Jesus Christ the holy One sent from God. He thought he had overthrown God's plans, but he did not know that he was merely playing into God's hands. He was a mere instrument in God's hands to actualize the plans that God had ordained for us from the foundation of the world.

Our salvation and our growing up into Christ's fullness and maturity is according to the unconquerable wisdom of God: *"...even the hidden wisdom which God ordained before the world unto our glory: which none of the princes of this world knew: for had they known it, they would not have crucified the Lord of glory"* (1 Corinthians 2:7-8).

Now through us, as we grow into Christ's fullness and stature, God is showing to the world, angels, Satan and all the hordes of hell that he, God, has the final say, and the last laugh. It is his counsel alone that will stand, for "there is no counsel or devise, or plan against God that can stand"[6].

Way Forward – Understudying Christ

Now that we know the plans and purposes of God for our lives, and the reason why he has brought us hitherto, what is the way forward? How can we actualize God's dream for our lives? How can we grow into the "fullness of the stature of Christ, unto a perfect man"? It is through understanding the life and character of Christ, so that we can grow up into his likeness. If we do not know him well enough, we can never grow to become like him. In other words, we must enrol in the "University of Christ." This "university" is not necessarily a university made up of four-walled buildings. It is another way of saying that we need to become "Disciples of Christ".

A disciple is a pupil, a trainee, a student, an apprentice; one who understudies another – his master – and trains to become like him… We need to study closely the life and teachings of Christ: his attitude, temperament, visions and goals. We need to know his thoughts, ways, manner of speech and action, and his overall ways of doing things – then we will endeavour to imitate him, or rather, allow him to work in our lives to replicate his nature, and do things his own way, through us.

Since he indwells us, and has promised to abide with us forever ("for it is God who works in us both to will and to do of his good pleasure" {Philippians 2:13}), we must study to become his oracles, his hands and feet, his representatives on earth. Indeed, Christ in us is our hope of glory.

As such, our transformation into his divine nature will come through the empowerment of His Holy Spirit residing in us. The Holy Spirit is our teacher, friend, guide, helper, senior partner, and Lord. As we commune with him in devoted prayers and fellowship, and study his word – the Bible – he will fashion us into his glorious image. In addition, we need to study to know the Christ of the Bible, and become his devoted disciples. We need to behold him and grow into his likeness, just as the scriptures prophesied:

> But we all, with open face beholding as in a glass the glory of the Lord, are changed into the same image from glory to glory, even as by the Spirit of the Lord (2 Corinthians 3:18).

> John said, "We shall be like him[7]".

> Peter said we are to "follow in his steps[8]".

> Paul said, "That I may know him[9]", and, "I press toward the mark of the high calling of God in Christ Jesus[10]".

To enable us apprehend him who first apprehended us, I have put together twenty-eight attributes of the person of Christ, which are revealed in the Scriptures. They are gems of priceless treasures designed to help every seeker to know better the Christ of the Bible. It is only when we truly know him and behold his glory that we will desire to become as he is, even in this world.

I therefore desire that you carefully read, study and assimilate every one of them, as by each of them you will be undergoing the mentorship of Christ. I also pray that each attribute shall be like a seed planted on the fruitful ground of your heart, helping you to become a true disciple of Christ: the Ultimate Disciple, in Jesus' name, Amen.

WORK BOOK

a) When did God ordain our salvation? What is the implication of *"before the foundation of the world"*? (Ephesians 1:5).

b) Explain God's unspeakable love to humanity. Can you practise it today to someone?

c) Try to explain *"the image of Christ."* Would you try to imitate him today?

d) Explain Transformation from the old nature to the new. Who can do it?

e) Explain how God's wisdom outsmarted that of the devil.

f) What is the University of Christ? Will you enrol? Who is the Teacher?

g) Summarize the message of this chapter in your own words.

Practical steps:

Seek some ways where you need transformation today. Do something new (Christ-like) that you have not been doing before.

Chapter Three

THE GREAT NEED FOR CHRISTIAN DISCIPLESHIP

From Babyhood to Maturity

The biblical definition of "Christian Discipleship" is the training of Christian believers to grow *"into the unity of the faith, and of the knowledge of the Son of God, unto a perfect man, unto the measure of the stature of the fullness of Christ."*[11] From Christ's point of view, this training is mandatory for all his followers. It is only by this process that, by the Spirit of God, a repented sinner transforms from his old worldly image into the very image and likeness of the Lord. Indeed, God's will is to grow us from being "babes in Christ" to "fathers".

Our growth or spirituality is not reckoned by our chronological age, and not even by the number of years we have known the Lord.

The main determinant of our spiritual attainment is the extent of our discipleship (the extent to which we have willingly put our necks to the yoke of Christ). And the Lord, talking about the need for us to be discipled, said that we should learn from him, that we should take his yoke upon us so we can learn to be meek and lowly in heart like himself[12].

Discipleship is not easy. It is yoking oneself to Christ, learning to live like him, and unlearning the ways of the world to which we have been so accustomed. It is not easy to be a disciple, and none of us can become the ultimate disciple overnight. However, we must start by recognizing the need for it and submitting to this discipline from the Lord. If we refuse to submit to the discipleship of the Lord we will end up behaving and living like unyoked oxen. And you cannot do much with them, until you put a yoke round their neck. It is only then that they can become productive for their owners. But the yoke of Christ is easy, and his burden is light for his beloved.

To the unsaved, God's command is *"Repent and be born-again"*. However, to those who have embraced Christ as Lord and Saviour, the Lord's command is *"Grow in grace, and in the knowledge of our Lord and Saviour, Jesus Christ"*[13]. We have no other choice but to grow, because we are either growing, or stagnating, or backsliding into the world. And God has no room for backsliders, except they repent and return to the Lord. God's desire is for us to grow into his fullness, with abundant Christ-like fruitfulness: otherwise he says he would cut us off from his vine-tree as unfruitful branches.

> *I am the true vine, and my Father is the husbandman. Every branch in me that beareth not fruit he taketh away; and every branch that beareth fruit he purgeth it, that it may bring forth more fruit… If a man abide not in me he is cast forth as a branch, and is withered, and men gather them, and cast them forth into the fire, and they are burned* (John 15:1,2,6).

These are strong words indeed from the Lord Jesus Christ himself, showing his determination to purge every newborn that he receives. He wants us purged from our old filthiness, and this comes through the process of discipleship. Notable exceptions to this rule would include the thief on the cross and others like him who died as soon after they repented, without opportunity for further spiritual growth.

Confirming the above, Apostle Paul said, *"Whom the Lord loveth, he chasteneth, and scourgeth every son whom he receiveth. If ye endure chastening, God dealeth with you as with sons, for what son is he whom the father chasteneth not? But if ye be without chastisement whereof all are partakers, then are ye bastards, and not sons"* (Hebrews 12:6-7).

The new birth is the foundation for our divine sonship; it is the fundamental requirement for our relationship with God. But after the new birth, God requires that we grow and mature gradually into the fullness of Christ's character and image. God does not expect us his children, to remain baby Christians, or carnal, worldly Christians indefinitely. He expects each one of us to desire more and more of Christ, and to *"apprehend that for which we were also apprehended by Christ"* (Philippians 3:12). We are expected to put away our props and crutches, and stand up, and walk straight and tall, with time. God expects us to put away the childish and foolish things of babyhood, and grow into children, then young adults, adult-Christians, and finally grow into mature Christians or "fathers"[14].

Dangerous Living at the Periphery of Grace

It is dangerous for a professed born-again child of God to continue to live a life that is inconsistent with the standards set by Christ for us. Carnal Christians are living at the outer fringes, or periphery of grace. That was where the fire of God's wrath started, as the children of Israel journeyed to the Promised Land (Numbers 11:1).

Our free salvation is secure only as we abide in the centre of God's will. If we stray out of his will and remain there, then we will not hold God accountable for the consequences of our carnality, stubbornness, or disobedience. He has promised to save to the uttermost all those who come to him through Christ. This means that God will do everything within his unlimited powers to save us from sin, Satan, and the world. But, we cannot hold him to ransom because of this promise if we become careless and self-indulgent in sin, and fail to discipline ourselves as he instructed us.

Hear what Paul said to the carnal Christians in Corinth:

> *Ye are yet carnal, for whereas there is among you envying, and strife, and divisions, are ye not carnal, and walk as men? ...know ye not that ye are the temple of God, and that the Spirit of God dwelleth in you? If any man defile the temple of God, him shall God destroy; for the temple of God is holy, which temple ye are* (1Corinthians 3:3, 16-17).

Brethren, it is as serious as that! Being a Christian, a born-again child of God, is the greatest privilege that can be bestowed upon any man on earth. It endows us with the hope of unspeakable glory and immortality in the coming kingdom of God... but it carries with it also an awesome responsibility: we are to grow into Christ's holiness, truth, faithfulness, equity, love, goodness and all the other divine attributes of God. We are to cast off all the sinful ways of the world that we followed in the past, and put on the new nature of Christ. It is very dangerous for us to continue to live after the pattern of the people of this world, whether they are in church, or outside of the church. God expects us to grow out of the primordial or elemental ruts of life in which we lived before he called us out of the world.

Discipleship is all about learning to *"...lift up the hands which hang down, and the feeble knees; and make straight paths for your feet, lest that which is lame be turned out of the way, but let it rather be healed"* (Hebrews 12:12-13).

Discipleship becomes very important to us when we understand both the severity and the abundant grace of God in his dealings with his people. Concerning this Paul said, *"I will therefore put you in remembrance, though ye once knew this, how that the Lord, having saved the people out of Egypt, afterward destroyed them that believed not"* (Jude 5).

Paul also stated that God baptized the Israelites as we were, and that they also drank the same spiritual drink as we do, and ate the same spiritual meat... but that with many of them God was not well pleased, and they were overthrown in the wilderness:

> *Now these things were our examples to the intent that we should not lust after evil things, as they also lusted, neither be ye idolaters... neither let us commit fornication,... neither let us tempt Christ, ...neither murmur ye, as some of them also murmured, and were destroyed by the destroyer"* (1 Corinthians 10:1-13).

The Benefits of Christian Discipleship

The Lord Jesus, having marvellously saved us by grace through his death and resurrection from the dead, is now working within us (by his Spirit) his unique work of grace. He is working to sanctify us wholly and make us fit candidates for heaven. He does not want us to enter heaven with the defiled garments of the world.

Paul's prayer for us is, "And the very God of peace sanctify you wholly; and I pray God your whole spirit, soul, and body be preserved blameless unto the coming of our Lord Jesus

Christ. Faithful is he that called you, who also will do it" (1 Thessalonians 5:23-24).

Discipleship commences when we realize God's purpose (his desire to purge, scourge, purify or sanctify us wholly), and we agree to engage and cooperate with the Holy Spirit in this work. Discipleship requires a willingness to learn, to train, and to put our necks to the yoke of Christ, which will produce for us the following benefits:

1. Growth in grace: For us to grow in grace and in the knowledge of our Lord Jesus Christ[15], we must submit more and more to the Lord's discipleship. Then will our profiting appear unto all.

2. Clearer knowledge of God's will: As we closely study the nature and attributes of Christ, we will have more of the mind of Christ, and we will receive a clearer picture of God's will in different areas of life.

3. Better self-evaluation: We will see more clearly our present estate in Christ, and discern any presumptuous sins in our lives.

4. Discipleship will help us to keep ourselves from the prophesied perilous times of the end-times. We will reject any form of godliness that lacks the power thereof[16].

5. We are chaste virgins of Christ. Discipleship will deliver us from falling into the same mould as the five unwise virgins whom God rejected at the marriage supper of the Lamb[17].

6. Closer fellowship with the Lord: *"Can two walk together except they be agreed?"* The more we yield to the Lord's discipleship, the more we too can become friends of God, like Abraham. And whatsoever we ask we receive

from the Lord, because we keep his commandments and do those things that are pleasing in his sight.

7. Confidence in the Day of Judgment: We will be bold on the Day of Judgment, *"...because as he is, so are we in this world"*[18].

The Call to Discipleship

From Genesis to Revelation the Bible is full of admonitions to Christians to grow in their faith (and this comes through Christian discipleship). We shall give only a few of such calls here:

Christ: *"Strive to enter in at the strait (narrow) gate; for many, I say unto you, will seek to enter in, and shall not be able (Luke 13:24).* As such he said, *"Be ye therefore perfect, even as your Father which is in heaven is perfect"* (Matthew 5:48).

Peter: *"...Give diligence to make your calling and election sure; for if ye do these things, ye shall never fall"* (2 Peter 1:10). He further said, *"For the time has come that judgment must begin at the house of God: and if it first begins at us, what shall the end be of them that obey not the gospel of Christ?"* (1 Peter 4:17).

Paul: *"I pummel my body and bring it under subjection, lest after that I have preached to others, I myself should be a castaway"* (1 Corinthians 9:27). *"If ye live after the flesh, ye shall die. But if ye through the Spirit do mortify the deeds of the body, ye shall live"* (Romans 8:13). Therefore, *"Study to show thyself approved unto God, a workman that need not to be ashamed, rightly dividing the word of God"* (2 Timothy 2:15); and *"go on to perfection"* (Hebrews 6:1).

John: *"Every man that hath this hope in him purifies himself, even as he is pure"* (1 John 3:3).

We are admonished to study the life and character of this "Jesus of Nazareth, a man approved of God among you by miracles and wonders and signs, which God did by him in the midst of you, as ye yourselves also know."[19]. As we study him, let us also seek to emulate him through the empowerment of the Holy Spirit, so that our lives will be patterned after him: for he is our perfect example, and he indwells us for this very purpose: that as he is in heaven, so we also might be in this world[20]; for *"we are members of his body, of his flesh, and of his bones"* (Ephesians 5:30) and *"in him we live, and move, and have our being"* (Acts 17:28).

Let Us Go on to Perfection

We have seen the great need for each one of God's children to manifest more of Christ to their world by developing more Christlike characters, and no longer conforming ourselves to the world's way of life. This is because from the foundation of the world, the Almighty God had fore-ordained and predestined that we would live in conformity with the image of Christ, so that we would inherit eternity and glory by his grace.

The book of Revelation strictly warns us that no man with defiled garments will be allowed entrance into that heavenly Jerusalem, the city of God[21]. Then the Spirit concludes in the last chapter of the Book:

> *Blessed are they that do his commandment, that they may have right to the tree of life, and may enter in through the gates into the city. For without are dogs, and sorcerers, and whoremongers, and murderers,*

21

and idolators, and whosoever loveth and maketh a lie
(Revelation 22:14-15).

Therefore, we must each undergo the circumcision of Christ (or his discipleship) in order to enter his kingdom. We must cast off our unclean garments of babyhood, and put on the robes of Christ's righteousness. We must grow in grace. This calls for us to critically re-examine ourselves and see if we have been taking our salvation for granted in any way, *"Let him that thinketh he standeth take heed, lest he fall."* We must search our lives and see areas where we need to make amends, and repent.

The best way we can assure ourselves of our right standing with God and our growth in his grace is to understudy Christ. He is our perfect law of liberty, and if we look at him through the mirror of the gospels and the epistles, if we see him as he is, then we also can grow into his fullness, growing *"from grace to grace, even as by the Spirit of the Lord".*

Paul said, *"I press toward the mark for the prize of the high calling of God in Christ Jesus."*

That should be our own mind-set also. Nevertheless, it is important to state here that although God has endued us with His blessed Holy Spirit to help us mortify the deeds of the flesh, to overcome Satan and the world, it is doubtful if any mortal man can ever attain to the fullness of Christ's perfection in this life. It is for this reason that the blood of Christ still speaks for us, and cleanses us from all sin (1 John 1:7-10). It is for this same reason that Christ Jesus, our Advocate, still makes intercession for us before the Father in heaven... But God expects us to seek daily to become more and more like Jesus, while we depend wholly on his grace and his finished work on the cross of Calvary for our eternal salvation (Eph. 2:8-10). Christ "is made unto us wisdom, and righteousness, and sanctification, and redemption" (1 Cor. 1:30).

Let us therefore with joy and enthusiasm behold him and his divine attributes, and emulate him who is Lord of all. Let us go on to perfection by studying the nature and attributes of our Lord Jesus Christ, who is our elder Brother.

WORK BOOK

a) Name the four stages of Christian growth, and describe the characteristics of each.

b) Why is discipleship not easy?

c) Is there any penalty for non-fruitfulness? Have you been purged or chastised by the Lord at any time? How can you recognize the Lord's chastisement?

d) Describe the more notable attributes of childhood, as seen in Christians.

e) Describe "life at the periphery of grace." What are the dangers? Is there any area you are living at the periphery of grace?

f) List some of the benefits of Christian discipleship.

g) What must you do in order to be discipled? Note some of the key words, "strive", "give diligence", etc.

h) Summarize the message of this chapter in your own words.

Practical steps:

Examine which areas of life you have been living at the "periphery of grace." Resolve today to move to a higher level. Make it a matter of priority and prayer.

Chapter Four

THE ATTRIBUTES OF CHRIST

In this chapter, we will present twenty-eight vital attributes of Christ's life, which if assimilated by the help of the Holy Spirit, would transform our lives into his own very divine nature.

SELF-REALISATION AND MISSION

Jesus, knowing that the Father had given all things into his hands, and knowing that he was come from God, and went to God... (John 13:3, 4).

They are not of the world, even as I am not of the world (John 17:16).

Thought: When the prodigal son realized himself, he stopped eating with the swine.

Christ Knew Himself

If we earnestly desire to be conformed to the image of Christ, we must know who we are in this world, just as Jesus knew who he was. If you do not know your identity and mission, you will follow the crowd to do evil. Knowing who you are will keep you focused. Jesus knew he was from above, and that the rest of the people were from below, of the earth, earthly.

Therefore, he sought only the things of heaven while on earth. He sought to establish heavenly principles on earth, and walked in heavenly ordinances. He did not allow earthly matters to become the preoccupation of his life. He left the mundane things of this world for worldly people to pursue: the inordinate pursuit of money and wealth, the quest for power, the hunger and appetite for more material things, earthly fame, etc. These have occupied humanity since the time of Adam; and Paul says that those things have drowned many and pierced them with sorrowful arrows ending in perdition[22]. Paul felt that having food and raiment we should be thereby satisfied, but make an earnest of the pursuit of godliness.

Again the Scripture declares that *"In the beginning was the Word, and the Word was with God, and the Word was God; the same was in the beginning with God. All things were made by him, and without him was not anything made that was made"* (John 1:1-3).

Christ knew all these, his divine Sonship, his Creatorship. Therefore, scriptures say that he did not seek honour of men. Jesus said, *"How can ye believe which seek honour one of another, and not the honour that comes from God only?"* Those who seek honours from fellow men will end up as men-pleasers.

We Are From Above, Not Of the World

We too, like Jesus are from above, through the new birth. We are in him (Christ), and he in us: we are one with him, and he is in God. Our lives are hid together in God[23]. We are citizens of heaven, and here (on earth) we have no abiding place. The fathers of faith, Abraham, Isaac and Jacob (and all the other heroes of faith) knew their citizenship was from heaven. They sought for a city, which hath foundations, whose builder, and maker is God[24]. Therefore, they lived on earth as pilgrims, and refused the diversionary allurements of this world, with its own standards and honours and values. They had a different set of values from the world, and sought their excellence in the things that God approved.

Recall that Jesus said we are in the world but not of the world. This statement is pregnant with meaning: Firstly, since we are in the world we cannot pretend that we are not in the world. We must meet with the world's people, trade, do business, interact with them, and relate to them: but we are to do so with all wisdom.

If we fail to interact and to relate, the world would pass us by and we would become irrelevant. Therefore we must receive this world's education, engage in the activities of the world, including sports, politics, business, etc. We should seek to excel in these things only as much as is possible for a pilgrim. They are not to become our major preoccupation, as it is for the world. The people of the world have no other hope. They believe that this is their only life and hope, so they must engage totally, even exclusively of any other ventures.

But for us it is not so! Why? Because Christ said that we are not of this world... *"We seek a kingdom to come."* Therefore though we are in the world, we know that we are citizens of a heavenly kingdom. We seek a better, more enduring kingdom. This worldly kingdom is soon coming to an end, but there is a heavenly kingdom coming soon to earth to replace this corruptible earthly kingdom. It is a prepared kingdom for prepared people, and no one with defiled garments will be allowed into it. Apostle Peter says, *"Seeing that ye have such hope, what manner of men ought ye to be in all holy conversation and godliness... wherefore... be diligent that ye may be found of him in peace, without spot and blameless*[25]*".*

Life Application

Friend, if you have been born-again of the Spirit of God, then you are a blood-bought bona-fide son of God with an eternal destiny to fulfil in God's kingdom. You can no longer live like ordinary folks, without vision and without hope; so, God expects you to be doing at least four things:

1. You are to live for the praise and glory of God. Your life of praise and worship to God Almighty will bring pleasure to heaven, because he created you for his praise.
2. God called you to walk in the steps of Christ, live in his exemplary righteousness, love and truth, and shine forth the knowledge of God into the world.
3. God has called us to preach the everlasting gospel of his coming kingdom in our entire world, and through this prepare the world for his coming.
4. Thus we are ordained to destroy the powers of hell holding men and women bondage in our world. We are to deliver our families, relations, friends, colleagues, cities and nations from darkness and from the evil sway of Satan and his hosts. We are to blow the trumpet of jubilee for them, as we await the return of the King of kings. Alleluia.

Friend, know who you are! You are a son of God, or a daughter of the King. Do not be carried away with the civilian affairs of this world, and forget that you are a prince of God, called for a purpose.

- You are from above, not from below.
- You are in the world, but not of the world.
- You have a priority assignment from God, which you must fulfil.

Know thyself, stay focused, and the Lord will give you a crown of life that will never fade away. Be sure you fulfil your

God-ordained mission to the world. And to do this, you must be filled with the Holy Spirit.

WORK BOOK

a) Who are you? Why do you say so?
b) Is everybody a child of God? Are there children of the devil? (1 John 3:8, 10)
c) What are the distinguishing features between the two?
d) What does God expect you to be doing which you are not yet doing?
e) Summarize the message of this chapter in your own words.

Practical steps:

Spend some time to meditate on the fact that you are not an earthly citizen, but an ambassador from heaven. You are here on a mission to rescue a lost world.

ATTRIBUTES OF CHRIST (2)

FILLED WITH THE HOLY SPIRIT

And Jesus, when he was baptized, went up straightway out of the water: and lo, the heavens were opened unto him, and he saw the Spirit of God descending like a dove, and lighting upon him (Matthew 3:16).

And Ananias...putting his hands on him (Saul) said... The Lord Jesus...hath sent me, that thou mightest receive thy sight, and be filled with the Holy Spirit (Acts 9:17).

Thought: If Christ (and the apostles) could do nothing without the Holy Spirit, who am I to try anything without him?

Christ, in fulfilling the will of his Father, depended wholly on the Holy Spirit of God, whom he had received from God. He knew that of his own self he could do nothing, but that through the Holy Spirit he could do all things. As such, Christ confessed that it was God the Father, in him, that did all the works, which he did[27].

Likewise, Paul said, "*I know that in my flesh dwelleth no good thing*", and, "*If you continue in the flesh, you shall die, but if you through the Holy Spirit mortify the deeds of the body, you shall* live"[28]. Thus Paul also depended wholly on the Holy Spirit to do the work that God called him to do.

Therefore, for us to emulate Christ, to grow into his fullness, and to do the works of Christ – for Christ to dwell fully in us, and work through us – we must seek the fullness of the Holy Spirit. The Holy Spirit is Christ within us[29]. He is the Spirit of the Father, proceeding from the Father. There is no way we can serve God with the arm of flesh. The arm of flesh will fail us. It is the Spirit that teaches, equips, empowers, works miracles, converts souls, sanctifies believers, and reveals the mind of Christ to us. It is he that recruits ministers to diverse ministries of the church.

Finally it is he, as the Lord of the church, that protects the church, broods on the church, and makes the church rapturable on the day of Christ. Everything pertaining to the life, ministry and future of the believer is wholly entrenched in the ministry of the indwelling Holy Ghost, for without him we can do nothing[30].

Life Application

In the light of Christ's total dependence on the Holy Spirit, it is evident that we ourselves cannot do anything without the Holy Spirit. He is God with us, in us, and working through our hands, feet, mouth, mind, and entire being, to reach to our world. Therefore, everyone who embraces Christ should seek the indwelling Holy Spirit, and receive him by faith. God is very willing to release his Holy Spirit to everyone that hungers and thirsts for him[31].

The only condition is true repentance from our sins, and belief in Christ our Saviour, as the Son of God. And we must trust God to release his Spirit to every penitent believer, since he has promised that in the new covenant he will come and dwell in us, and walk in us, and we shall be his people, and he will be our God[32]. If we believe his promise and his great faithfulness to his word, we will have no reason to doubt him when we ask him to fill us with his Spirit.

It is also important to note that God does not expect us to be perfect before he gives us his Holy Spirit. He gives the Holy Spirit to imperfect people who are of a contrite penitent heart, who believe his promises and who obey him.

Scripturally, the Holy Spirit is usually given at water baptism, with the laying on of hands and prayers, by an ordained and Spirit-filled minister of Christ. However, God reserves the privilege to pour out of himself on any believer at any time of his choice. For example, when Peter was ministering to the Gentiles at the house of Cornelius the centurion, God poured out his Spirit, before Peter could conclude his message. The ritual of water baptism followed after; teaching us that the apostles deemed water baptism to be important, and not to be omitted.

Paul made sure that all those who heard him, who believed in Christ, received the in-filling with the Holy Spirit. When he met with the Ephesian Christians, he asked them pointedly, *"Did you receive the Holy Spirit when you believed?"* When they responded in the negative, he baptized them in water and then laid hands on them, and they received the Holy Spirit with evidence of speaking in tongues[33].

In Samaria, after the great evangelistic campaign of Phillip, when Peter arrived and found that the believers had not received the Holy Spirit, (even though they had been baptized), he laid hands on them, and prayed for them, and they received the Holy Spirit (Acts 8:14-17).

Dear friend, if you have not received the Holy Spirit, please ask God, seek this gift, for you will surely receive. *"For the promise is for you and your children and those afar off, as many as the Lord will call"* (Acts 2:39).

In conclusion, it is imperative that everyone who embraces Christ as Lord and Saviour should ensure that he receives the Holy Spirit. The Holy Spirit will only come on invitation, by a believer who has repented, shown genuine sorrow for his sins, and determined to turn away from his sins to obey the Lord. As he submits to the ordinance of baptism[34], and is prayed for by a man of God filled with the Holy Spirit, the Holy Spirit will surely fall on such a believer, often with manifestations, e.g. speaking in tongues or prophesying. Certainly one sure sign of his indwelling is the power to live the crucified life in Christ.

WORK BOOK

a) Who is the Holy Spirit? What does he do for the believer? Explain.

b) Christ and the apostles could do nothing without the Holy Spirit. Have you been operating without him?

c) Have you been baptized by immersion (like Christ)? On the other hand, were you baptized in any other way? Explain.

d) Have you ever spoken in tongues?

e) What gifts of the Spirit do you have, if any?

f) Summarize the message of this chapter in your own words.

Practical steps:

Ask your mentor to direct you to a minister of Christ (possibly in your church) who can guide you into the fullness of the Holy Spirit and power of God. However, be sure you have had water baptism.

A MAN OF SORROWS AND ACQUAINTED WITH GRIEF

He is despised and rejected of men; a man of sorrows, and acquainted with grief: and we hid as it were our faces from him; he was despised, and we esteemed him not (Isaiah 53:3).

I say the truth in Christ; I lie not, my conscience also bearing me witness in the Holy Ghost, that I have great heaviness and continual sorrow in my heart. For I could wish that myself were accursed from Christ for my brethren, my kinsmen according to the flesh: Who are Israelites; to whom pertaineth the adoption, and the glory, and the covenants, and the giving of the law, and the service of God, and the promises; Whose are the fathers, and of whom as concerning the flesh Christ came, who is over all, God blessed forever. Amen (Romans 9:1-5).

The sacrifices of God are a broken spirit: a broken and a contrite heart, O God, thou wilt not despise (Psalm 51:17).

Thought: We are not broken, because we do not yet know God's holiness.

Although Christ never committed any sin from his virgin birth until his crucifixion, yet Isaiah prophesied that he was *"a man of sorrows".* His sorrow was for our own sins, our transgressions against God and his holy laws. He bore our iniquities, not just when they crucified him, but throughout his life, he made intercession for our sins. In a sense, he took our sins from cradle to the cross for he was born to die for the sins of the world. The cross was the culmination of his sin-bearing mission in the world.

The weight of the sins of erring humanity weighed heavily in the mind of Christ. There was no blot, no blemish, no iniquity found on him, yet he pleased not himself on this account, because, *"the reproaches of those that reproached thee fell on me."*

The spirit of repentance is one of the greatest attributes of any child of God who wants to continue any dealings with God. No matter how holy our walk with God may have been, we must always *"rejoice with trembling."*[35] Why tremble? Because without God's constant help we will fail miserably; our walk with him depends purely on his grace, and even then, we may never really attain to Christ's perfection in this life, but his grace is our covering. We depend entirely on his righteousness, not ours.

All of God's great saints remonstrated with God on their inadequacies, and so must we:

Abraham slipped in his quest for a child, and slept with Hagar.

Job, attested by God as the most righteous man of his generation, confessed, *"I have heard of thee by the hearing of the ear, but now my eye seeth thee; wherefore I repent in dust and ashes"* (Job 42:5-6).

Prophet Isaiah declared, *"Woe is me, for I am undone; for I am a man of unclean lips dwelling in the midst of a people of unclean lips"* (1 Timothy 1:15).

Paul confessed that he was the chief of sinners. "...*Christ Jesus came into the world to save sinners; of whom I am chief*" (1 Timothy 1:15). Note, "I am".

Peter *"was to be blamed"* (Galatians 2:11).

Thus it is evident that "there is none righteous, no, not one." We must all depend on grace for our justification, and that should keep us humble.

Life Application

i) We must never lose sight of our frailty. We must be of a humble and contrite spirit continually both because of our own human nature and tendency to sin, and because of the sins of the multitude of people around us.

ii) A broken and contrite heart is well pleasing to God, but also helps us to be careful to avoid every appearance of sin around us. If we become proud, we could live with grievous and presumptions sins without being aware of them (like David after he caused Uriah's death).

Is it not true that many born-again Christians still tell lies, commit fornication, are unforgiving, steal, cheat, and commit many other vices? Why then should we not be sober and repentant in our walk with God? God resists the proud, but gives grace to the humble ones.

May God grant us all a broken and contrite heart, in Jesus' name, Amen!

> *Oh that my head were waters, and mine eyes a fountain of tears, that I might weep day and night for the slain of the daughter of my people!* (Jeremiah 9:1)

WORK BOOK

a) Explain this Scripture, *"Rejoice with trembling"* (Psalm 2:11).

b) Contrast between *"Sacrifice"* and *"Brokenness"* by explaining Psalm 51:16, 17.

c) Do some people try to cover their sins by making some sacrifice? What should they rather do?

d) Do you ever mourn and sigh on behalf of sinners? (Ezekiel 9:4).

e) Summarize the message of this chapter in your own words.

Practical steps:

Godly sorrow works repentance (2 Corinthians 7:9-10). Pray that God will reveal to you areas where you need to show genuine sorrow in your life, or in the lives of your loved ones because of sin. Then repent today.

A PERFECT AND SINLESS LIFE

He was manifested to take away our sins, and in him is no sin. Whosoever abideth in him sinneth not. Whosoever sinneth hath not seen him, neither known him" (1 John 3:5-6).

For even hereunto were ye called: because Christ also suffered for us, leaving us an example that ye should follow his steps: who did no sin, neither was guile (deceit) found in his mouth: who when he was reviled, reviled not again; when he suffered he threatened not, but committed himself to him that judgeth righteously... (1 Peter 2:21-24).

He that committeth sin is of the devil...Whosoever is born of God doth not commit sin; for his seed remaineth in him: and he cannot sin, because he is born of God (1 John 3:9).

Thought: Fools think sin is unconquerable; but we are more than conquerors through the indwelling Christ in us.

Christ lived a life free of sin. Yet he said that of himself he could do nothing. It was the Father that dwelt in him that did the works.

The same Holy Spirit that dwelt in Christ now dwells in us his disciples. That is why he told his disciples, *"Be ye therefore perfect, even as your Father in heaven is perfect."*[37]. But if we think we cannot live a sinless and perfect life by the power of God's Spirit, why then did Christ command that we should follow his steps? And why did God command Abraham, and say, *"I am God Almighty; walk before me and be thou perfect"* (Genesis 17:1). No wonder, Paul said, *"Let us go on to perfection"* (Hebrews 6:1) and *"...we wish, even your perfection"* (2 Corinthians 13:9).

Therefore, *"...let us cleanse ourselves from all filthiness ...perfecting holiness in the fear of God"* (2 Corinthians 7:1); so we must *"let patience have her perfect work, that ye may be perfect, and entire, wanting nothing"* (James 1:4). To achieve this, God has also committed himself to making *"you perfect, establish, strengthen, settle you"* (1 Peter 5:10). If you let him, the God of peace will *"make you perfect in every good work"* (Hebrews 13:20-21). *"All Scripture is given by inspiration of God... that the man of God may be perfect"* (2 Timothy 3:16, 17).

It is thus abundantly clear from all the scriptures quoted above that God delights in us living holy and blameless lives. He wants to make us perfect and without sin. He wants us to emulate Christ, and to walk in his steps. God hates sin, and has paid a heavy price once and for all for sins, and he does not want us to be entangled any more with sin.

In fact he has graciously covered us with Christ's garment of righteousness, and does not want any spot or blemish on it. And to ensure this he has also reserved Christ's blood in his heavenly altar to wash us from every blemish or spot that we may encounter in our lives' pilgrimage. And thirdly, he has given us his blessed Holy Spirit to live within us forever, to help us, sanctify us, and equip us to live holy lives before him all the days of our lives.

Life Application

i) Like Apostle Paul, let us also press towards the mark of living lives free from sin, by grace, through the enablement of God's Holy Spirit. And continually say, *"That I may know him, and the power of his resurrection... Not as though I had already attained, either were already perfect: but I follow, after, if that by any means I may apprehend that for which also I am apprehended of Christ Jesus. Brethren I count not myself to have apprehended: but this one thing I do, forgetting those things that are behind, and reaching forth to those things that are before, I press towards the mark of the high calling of God in Christ Jesus. Let us therefore, as many as be perfect, be thus minded..."* (Philippians 3:12-15).

What a glorious quest! The apostle of righteousness by grace is running with his gift of righteousness. He is obeying the scripture that says, *"Work out your own salvation with fear and trembling, for it is God that works in you both to will, and to do of his own pleasure."*[38] He wanted Christ's righteousness to be seen in his life. He did not want to appear as if he had received the grace of God in vain.

Likewise, we also must bear the fruit of righteousness abundantly, and seek Christ's perfect and sinless nature displayed in our lives, even as he lives within us. Let us heed the voice of the Holy Spirit speaking within us, who will lead us always to do that which is right before God and men.

ii) The quest for fullness of Christian maturity (Christian perfection) is not just for a few selected individuals. The Bible commends that it should be the corporate goal of the entire Body of Christ. That is why the Lord gave gifts of ministers to the church, *"For the perfecting of the saints... till we all come in the unity of the faith, and of the knowledge of the Son of God, unto a perfect man, unto the measure of the stature of the fullness of Christ"* (Ephesians 4:12-13).

iii) Is there anything beclouding our picture of living a perfect and sinless life for God? Is there any high thing or sin threatening us in running with this vision? Whatever it is, let us put it out of the way, and seek this fruit, this worthy goal that God has given us to pursue. Yes, we are already made righteous by the gift of Christ's righteousness by faith. Nevertheless, we are encouraged to come into full manifestation of the same, an experiential knowledge of his righteousness; for it is God who works in us, both to will, and to do, of his own good pleasure, Amen.

WORK BOOK

a) Explain: *"...Whosoever sinneth hath not known him"* (1 John 3:6).

b) Where and how do we derive our righteousness as believers in Christ?

c) Explain Ephesians 4:12-13. What is God's vision for us? Is that your own vision?

d) Summarize the message of this chapter in your own words.

Practical steps:

Resolve today, as an agent of God's righteousness wrought in Christ Jesus, to live a sinless and perfect life today, through the empowerment of the Holy Spirit. If it does not work today, if you offend in thought, word, or deed then try again tomorrow. Practise living out Christ's righteousness through prayer and diligent application, while standing solidly on his righteousness already imputed to you by grace through faith (Romans 4:6-8, 9:30).

INWARD AND OUTWARD PURITY

May the very God of peace sanctify you wholly. And I pray God that your whole spirit, soul, and body be preserved blameless unto the coming of our Lord Jesus Christ (1 Thessalonians 5:23).

Whosoever looks on a woman to lust after her has committed adultery with her already in his heart. And if thy right eye offends thee, pluck it out, and cast it from thee... (Matthew 5:28-29).

Thought: You will shudder at the base cravings in the hearts of some of our best men.

Christ lived a life of wholesome purity, inwardly and outwardly, and so must we. However, many of us find it easier to embrace some truths, and even preach them, than to do them. The Pharisees, the religious leaders of Christ's day, believed many scriptural truths, and even taught them, but they could not do them. Outwardly, they professed their religiosity, but inwardly they were ravenous wolves, as their acts showed. Even though they looked for a Messiah, when he appeared they killed him because of envy.

The same thing could happen to us. We can claim to belong to Christ, and go through the rituals of Christianity, but if we do not take the trouble to discipline our inward motives and desires, we would be pursuing a vain religion before God. We could easily become one of the hypocrites in church, without realizing it. We need the help of God in this matter of worshipping God "in spirit, and in truth".

Christianity of the Heart

Christ warned his listeners that *"Out of the hearts proceed evil thoughts, adulteries, fornications, thefts, false witness and blasphemies. These are the things which defile a man"* (Matthew 15:19). Therefore, if we desire to be true worshippers who worship God in spirit and in truth, we must watch our hearts (to search and root out from within our hearts every sinful thought, desire or motive). That is where true worship, true Christianity, starts.

For example, Christ taught us that whosoever looks on a woman with lust has already committed adultery with her in his heart. Likewise, whosoever hates his brother in his heart has committed murder against him already in his heart. In addition, whosoever speaks evil, and calls his brother, "Vain fellow", or "Fool", is in danger of judgment and hell-fire (Matthew 5:22).

Therefore, in our quest to know God better, and attain Christ's perfection, we must go deeper in our search, and in our worship of him. While depending fully and entirely on Christ's righteousness, we must also seek the help of the Holy Spirit to put to death within us, all workings of the flesh and worldliness, which we inherited from the world around us[39]. We must cooperate with the Holy Spirit in casting *"down imaginations and everything that exalts itself against the knowledge of God in our lives, and to bring into captivity every thought to the obedience of Christ."*[40]

Life Application

We must address these three focal areas in our desire to live well-pleasing lives in the spirit, soul and body unto God.

i) **Purify your Thoughts:** God says, *"...I am he which searcheth the reins and hearts, and I will give unto every one of you according to your works"* (Revelation 2:23)."*The LORD seeth not as man seeth, for man looketh on the outward appearance, but the LORD looketh on the heart"* (1 Samuel 16:7b; Acts 1:24).

This means that we should properly always evaluate our hearts' intentions, motives, values, desires, etc. And since what we think often depends on what we see and hear and feel, we must also be careful of what we watch and hear on TV, radio, and internet. We must evaluate what we hear and read, and the company we keep and so on. Do not let your heart stray after the half-naked men or women we see around us, or on your TV screen. Do not allow your heart to be provoked to carnal lusting by the worldliness around you. Keep yourself pure for God, and have the courage to tune off. Remember that David's sin was as a result of what he saw.

Cast down unwholesome thoughts and imaginations before they take root in your mind.

ii) **Purify your Words:** Christ wants you to be his oracle, his mouthpiece. He does not want us to defile ourselves by the words we speak. He said, "By your words you shall be justified, and by your words you shall be condemned."[41] Indeed, he does not want us to allow the devil to hijack our tongues to speak evil words. Our words should always be *"words of grace, seasoned with salt, ministering grace, life and health to the hearers"*. Apostle James testifies that *"if any man offends not in word, the same is a perfect man, and able also to bridle the whole body"*[42].

Therefore if we desire to be true disciples of the Lord we must take heed to the teachings of scriptures, and be *"swift to hear, but slow to speak, and slow to wrath."* Let us restrain our tongues from speaking lies and mischief, and from criticizing and condemning other people. Instead let us learn to pray for others.

The tongue, admits apostle James, is a small member with vicious powers to destroy others, and finally it will be set on fire of hell. No wonder the prophet Isaiah exclaimed, *"Woe is me, for I am undone; for I am a man of unclean lips, dwelling in the midst of a people of unclean lips: For my eyes have seen the King, the Lord of hosts"* (Isaiah 6:5). May we all be privileged to see the Lord, too, in Jesus' name, Amen!

iii) **Purify your Actions**: *"Lord, who shall abide in thy tabernacle? Who shall dwell in thy holy hill? He that walketh uprightly, and worketh righteousness, and speaketh the truth in his heart"* (Psalm 15:1).

Christ said that he is the light of the world, and whosoever does righteousness will come to him so that his works will be made manifest in his light. God wants our deeds to be done with integrity, honour and transparency. He hates the hidden works of darkness. He hates intrigues and craftiness. Christ never told a lie, nor did he deal in falsehood. And we are called to emulate him in our dealings with people and with God. There are many who would like to be Disciples of Christ, but you can never be sure of their words.

You cannot be sure, when they are telling you the truth; you can never be sure if there is any hidden agenda in their promises or their dealings. God wants us to be free of craftiness, so let your *"'yea' be yea, and your 'no', no."*

Christ was meek, gentle and harmless like a dove, and he taught us to follow his example. He said we are God's sheep and lambs; why then are many of us violent and quarrelsome? Why do we shout and strive with other people? Where then is the meekness of Christ? We must not forget that *"the wisdom that is from above is first pure, then peaceable, gentle and easy to be entreated, full of mercy and good fruits, without partiality, and without hypocrisy. And the fruit of righteousness is sown in peace of them that make peace"* (James 3:17-18).

Therefore, our actions should always be guided by the law of peace and gentleness and mutual consideration, if we are to be the true disciples of Christ. May the Lord help us to yield our members (our bodies) to the Lordship of Christ, in Jesus' name, Amen!

WORK BOOK

a) Explain: When does "looking" or admiration turn to "lusting" (evil desire)?

b) What caused David's downfall? If you were in David's shoes and had the power to take the woman, what would you have done? Would you have invited her to your home?

c) How easy has it been for you to control the imaginations of your heart? How can it be done effectively? Remember, "Prevention is better than cure", so what can be done to prevent wrong thoughts (e.g. sexual lust) from lodging in your heart?

d) Do you call some people "idiots", "fools", etc.? What is the consequence of this on Judgment Day? (Matt 5:22).

e) Summarize the message of this chapter in your own words.

Practical step:

Determine today not to allow any defiled thought to lodge in your heart. Make a practice of prayerfully casting down and rebuking such imaginations for one week, and then review your effort. Stop calling people "fools", "idiots", etc.

ATTRIBUTES OF CHRIST (6)

GREAT HUMILITY

But (Christ) made himself of no reputation, and took upon him the form of a servant, and was made in the likeness of man (Philippians 2:7).

Humble yourselves therefore under the mighty hand of God, that he may exalt you in due time (1 Peter 5:6; James 4:10).

Thought: You can lift up someone who is down, but the only way to help someone who is puffed up is to deflate him.

Christ was the most humble man that ever lived. Even though heaven and earth and everything in them was made by him; though he was the Son of God and therefore God himself; though he enjoyed eternal privileges as God's Son in the bosom of his Father; though he made the angels and all mankind... at the time appointed of the Father, the scriptures declare that Christ did not think equality with God something to hold onto. Rather he *"emptied himself (made himself of no reputation) and took upon himself the form of a servant, and was made in the likeness of men. And being found in fashion as a man, he humbled himself, and became obedient unto death, even the death of the cross"* (Philippians 2:7-8).

Christ, the God-man made himself lower than God, lower than angels, and even as a man, he made himself as a servant, even as a criminal (which he was not), in order to fulfil the will of the Father.

Christ taught a lot on the virtue of humility, and his life was the epitome of humility. Christ was humility personified. He believed in serving others. He did not wait to be served. He taught us that those who served others were the greatest in the kingdom of God. At the Last Supper, when supper ended, he took off his clothes, and girded himself with a towel, and poured out water in a bowl and washed the feet of all his disciples. As he washed their feet stooping down before them, he also wiped their feet with the towel with which he was girded[43]. What an act of humility! And he said that this was how we are to humble ourselves and serve one another in love.

Extreme Humility Attracts Extreme Elevation

In his great humility, Christ did not open his mouth to defend himself when he was brought to the judgment hall of Pilate and Herod. Rather, as a sheep that is dumb, he allowed his judgment to be taken away, so that God's will would be done in his life. Even though he had power to call upon the Father throughout his travail (and the Father would have dispatched more than twelve legions of angels to rescue him), in his humility he did not use those powers.

Even while on the cruel cross, and in agonizing pains, he remained meek and humble. He did not use the occasion of such gross injustice to pronounce a curse or railing accusation against the perpetrators of that wicked act. Rather he emptied himself and carried the shame and sin of all mankind. And for that reason God finally raised him from the dead, and exalted him to his own right hand, and gave him a name that is above all names; that at the name of Jesus every knee should bow, and every tongue confess that Jesus is Lord to the glory of the Father. Show me any truly great man of God, and I will show you a man who has learnt and assimilated the humility of Christ.

Great Men, Humble Disposition

Speaking of Moses, one of the greatest men of God that ever lived, the scriptures said he was *"meek, above all the men that were upon the face of the earth"* (Numbers 12:3). When accused by Aaron and Miriam of marrying an Ethiopian woman, the Bible said he did not answer them back... rather, it was God who defended him.

Peter, who in his earlier days violently used the sword to cut off a man's ear in defence of Christ, later became so humble that he would willingly give himself up to be crucified upside down for Christ. Paul the apostle, who violently supervised the stoning of Stephen to death, became so humble that he willingly suffered greatly for Christ, without regrets. In addition, even though he received visions of heaven while alive, and wrote most of the New Testament books, yet he described himself as *"less than the least of all saints."*

Abraham the father of faith showed great humility in his dealings with Lot his younger nephew. Even though he was the one called by God, and was old enough to be the father of Lot, when dispute arose between his herdsmen and Lot's herdsmen, Abraham asked Lot to divide the land of inheritance, and to choose first. This sounds very unfair to himself, but in humility, and to avoid strife, he allowed it to be so... and Lot chose what appeared to be the best portion: the well-watered land of Sodom (which later proved to be a disastrous choice).

Even Joseph, the son of Jacob, showed great humility when he met with his wicked brothers who had sold him into slavery in Egypt. Instead of taking revenge, he wept for them, and provided the land of Goshen for them and their children.

Life Application

In order to be able to accomplish the mission that God has for us in this world, we too, like Christ, must humble ourselves greatly. We must earnestly seek to inculcate within us the mind of Christ, and seek his great humility. When we stop fighting for ourselves, then God will arise to fight for us, because he is the God of vengeance. When we allow ourselves, in humility before God, to be rather defrauded instead of fighting back, then God will arise for us. And when men curse us, and we bless them rather, then God will arise to bless us.

When we are thrown into a pit because of our profession of Christ, and we do not fight back, then God will arise for us - as he did for Joseph and take us from the pit to the palace. God's power is unlimited, and his eyes run to and fro throughout the earth to show his awesome might on behalf of those whose hearts are perfect toward him. After Lot had chosen the better portion of the land of Canaan (by human standards), God came to Abraham, and told him to view the whole land of Canaan eastward, westward, northward, and southwards. *"For all the land which thou seest, to thee will I give it, and to thy seed forever"* (Genesis 13:15). This included the portion which Lot had acquired by his covetousness. If we humble ourselves before the Lord, in due time, the Lord will lift us up.

Furthermore, the scriptures admonish us to submit to our elders, to our parents, to those in authority, wives to their own husbands, and all of us to one another in love. May God crown us with this great virtue, as Disciples of Christ, in Jesus' name Amen!

WORK BOOK

a) What does it mean when scripture says that Christ made himself of no reputation?

b) Some Christians serve others with pride. Explain this ironical statement. Can we serve and still be proud?

c) Give some scriptural examples of men of God who showed great humility. Is there any living example?

d) God resists the proud, but gives grace to the humble (James 4:6; 1 Peter 5:5), explain this.

e) Summarize the message of this chapter in your own words.

f) Why did Abraham ask Lot to divide the land and choose first? Give possible reasons. Which is the most plausible? Can we emulate him?

g) What should Lot have done? Give possible options open to Lot, and choose the best.

Practical steps:

Try to render humble service today to at least two or three people. Try it again tomorrow, and keep at it for one month, then review your progress. Do not do it to be seen of men.

ATTRIBUTES OF CHRIST (7)

FAITH IN GOD

*Now faith is the substance (confidence) of things hoped
for; the evidence of things not seen. For by it the elders
obtained a good report* (Hebrews 11:1-2).

Faith is the indispensable requirement we all need to please
God in our walk with him. *"If thou wouldest believe, thou
shouldest see the glory of God"* (John 11:40).

Thought: Start with the rod in your hand to divide your mighty
Red Sea. God will only come in when you have started.

Christ had great faith in God, while on earth he showed it in
all his dealings (both with men and with devils). Through his
faith in God, he did mighty miracles, wrought wonders, and
delivered many sick folk and cast out oppressing demons. In
all his temptations and trials, his faith in God never wavered.

There were times of great crises in his life e.g. when he
was tempted by Satan after a gruesome 40-day fast, and when
he was brutally attacked and nailed on the cross by Pilate's
soldiers and others, but in all these his faith held firmly to
God. There were times he could no longer understand what
God was doing, for example when God the Father departed
from him as he carried the full weight of the sins of the world

on himself at the cross. Although perplexed by this act of his Father–God, yet he reposed complete confidence in him, as a God who only did righteousness. He cried out, *"My God, my God, why hast thou forsaken me?"* Then he concluded, *"Into Thy hands I commit my Spirit"*.

He also taught his disciples to *"Have faith in God"* (Mark 11:22), and that *"All things are possible to him that believes."* He told Martha that if she would believe she would see the glory of God[44], a good admonition for all of us also. When the disciples failed to show faith, and could not deliver a child that was possessed with a convulsing spirit, Christ was very displeased, and called all those involved a "faithless and perverse generation" (Matthew 17:17). However, when men showed faith in God, Jesus gave them high commendations[45].

The disciples asked the Lord to increase their faith. Thereafter, they went about doing great signs and wonders in their work for God. Through this, they fulfilled the word that Christ had prophesied, that his disciples would do greater works than he had done.

Faith's Good Report

The scriptures plainly declare, *"Without faith it is impossible to please God. For he that comes to God must believe that God is, and that he is a rewarder of those who diligently seek him."* It is by faith that the elders obtained a good report from God, and so it is evident that without it we ourselves cannot obtain any good report from God.

Through faith, Abel offered unto God a 'more excellent' sacrifice, and because of that sacrifice, although he died, scriptures declare that he still lives... He will come up in the first resurrection. Noah also lived a life of righteousness in the midst of a perverse world corrupted by sin and Satan. He did not follow the multitude to commit iniquity because he believed that no matter how long it took, God would one day judge the world of their evil deeds. And so he prevailed over the flood that consumed the rest of humanity.

Abraham had such faith in God that when asked to leave his mother, father, brethren and country to an unknown country, he obeyed and left, *"not knowing whither he went"*. He just trusted God to lead him somehow; he went prayerfully with blind faith, until God brought him to the land of Canaan. Even in the land of Canaan, when God desired him to offer up his only begotten son Isaac for a burnt offering, Abraham did not refuse God. He was ready to do it, and was in the act of doing it, when God intervened and stopped him. Because of that act of obedience by faith, God sealed all the promises he had made to him by an everlasting oath.

It is by the same faith in God that many missionaries left their native countries to go on missions to cruel heathen nations where many of them laid down their lives for Christ. By their faithful obedience, they brought nations under subjection to Christ, and wrote their names in gold in God's book of records.

Life Application

It is imperative for us who are yet alive today to desire, seek, and manifest that same faith which Christ and his apostles and the elders of faith showed in their own dispensation. Without this faith, we can do nothing worthwhile for God in our generation. We must come to know God as the Lord of the Universe, the invisible God who controls the entire universe and his creation, whose eyes run to and fro throughout the earth to show his awesome strength for his people.

Daniel trusted in this God and refused the dainty meat and wine of king Nebuchadnezzar that were first offered to idols. He refused to bow down to the gods of this king, and even though they threw him into the den of lions, God did an incredible miracle for him and delivered him.

Let us learn to repose our full trust in this great and mighty God whom we profess to serve through his Son. He is worthy of our obedience, and mighty to save to the uttermost those who trust in him. And even if he is not pleased to deliver us in his own wisdom, let us fully be committed to him, and be ready, if need be, to lay down our lives for him who also is able to raise us up even from the dead on the last day.

Faith Will Prevail

Trust him to save your troubled marriage, and keep praying and doing well even in the worst of times. Trust him to provide healing even in the worst of circumstances. Stand on his word, declare it, and keep trusting him. Entrust your life, your business, your circumstances, your ministry, and everything you own into his hands. Keep doing what is right, praying fervently for his intervention, and God will never abandon his own. God is intrinsically a faith-God, for he has chosen to remain invisible to us, and only relates to us through the medium of faith.

If we choose to neglect our faith, we will lose touch with him; but if we build up our most holy faith then we can feel him with the hands of faith, and he will reach out to us too. God will surely show up, and on time, one way or the other, to show you that he never abandons those who put their trust in him. Our God is a caring God, a faithful Father, and he will arise for you if you put your faith in him.

Has God given you a task to undertake for him? Do it in faith. Believe that he will help you to accomplish it. God's tasks are usually greater than we can handle by ourselves, but if we believe in our God, he will help us handle it. Has God given you an errand to run for him? Then go in faith. He will assign angels and men to go with you. He has a thousand ways to accomplish that task that you do not know about.

Has God sent you to deliver a message for him? Then do it fearlessly, for God will help you. He will be with you, and speak through your mouth. Have faith in God, it is the indispensable requirement for exploits in his kingdom. If need be, ask him for more faith. Nevertheless, by all means, move forward, and cross your Red Sea. For every assignment that God gives a man, he will make a way where there is no way. Faith in God will pull down the mountains on your way. Start obeying him, start doing what he says you should do. Help is on the way as you labour in faith with fervent prayers. Thus says the Lord:

"...*Speak unto the children of Israel that they go forward*" (Exodus 14:15).

WORK BOOK

a) Define faith biblically; then in your own words.
b) What proofs do you have for the existence of God? State five of them.
c) Why do you think God has chosen to remain invisible? After the resurrection, why did Christ not show himself to the scribes, Pharisees and the entire Jewish nation?
d) How does faith originate? How can we develop more faith?
e) Describe the faith actions of seven men of faith in Hebrews 11.

f) Why is faith for miracles not given to every Christian? What must you do if you need it?

g) Summarize the message of this chapter in your own words.

Practical steps:

Is there anything that God told you to do, but you have been afraid to start it? Pray and start it now. Don't procrastinate it.

LOVE FOR GOD

Then one of them… asked him a question, tempting him and saying, Master, which is the great commandment in the Law? Jesus said unto him: Thou shalt love the Lord thy God with all thy heart and with all thy soul, and with all thy mind. This is the first and great commandment. And the second is like unto it, Thou shall love thy neighbour as thyself. On these two commandments hang all the law and the prophets (Matthew 22:35-40).

For this is the love of God that we keep his commandments; and his commandments are not grievous (1 John 5:3).

Thought: No parent would be flattered by a child's affirmations of love when the house chores are still left undone.

Christ taught his disciples that the greatest commandment in the Law was to love God, and that this love is demonstrated through obedience to God and his Laws. It was of no use calling him *"Lord, Lord"*, and yet flouting his commands. And we are to love God above everyone else, and everything else.

Christ obviously loved his Father–God more than any man or woman, and more than what the world (or Satan) had to offer. Christ loved his Father–God more than even his own very life. He demonstrated this love when Peter tried to dissuade him from going to Jerusalem to die on the cross for the sins of humanity. Christ was so irked by Peter's effrontery in trying to dissuade him, that he called Peter, "Satan": *"Get thee behind me, Satan; thou art an offence unto me; for thou savourest not the things that be of God, but those things that be of men"* (Matthew 16:23). He knew Satan was behind those words.

True Love Demonstrated through Obedience

Christ taught his disciples that true love of God was to keep God's commandments. He had exemplified this love by keeping all of God's commandments, even to the point of laying down his life for the sins of the world. He exemplified his love for God by living a life free from all sin. Because of Christ's love for the Father, he disregarded all of Satan's offers for self-aggrandisement, self-promotion, and pursuit of all unlawful self-pleasing desires. Christ demonstrated his love further by the following:

- He was in constant fellowship and communion with the Father through the communion of the Holy Spirit.
- He prayed always without fainting.
- He did always those things that were well-pleasing to the Father.
- He praised and thanked God always, giving him constant adoration, worship, and reverence. He feared the Father.[46]
- He loved the people around him, even his enemies.

Jesus accused the Pharisees of showing much love with their tongues, but that they failed to keep God's commandments. As such, he said that they were worshipping God in vain[47].

The Disciples of Christ taught their followers likewise, and maintained that true love of God is to keep his commandments. This obedience to God ensured God's divine presence and favour continually upon his people. No wonder all the disciples obeyed him unto death; *"They loved not their lives unto the death"*[48].

They believed and taught their followers that obedience to God, the fear of God, and the practice of righteousness and truth, together with loving one another as he taught us were the hallmarks of the love of God, and would lead those who practised it into eternal life, by grace.

Life Application

A true disciple of the Lord would love Christ, and love God, just as Christ admonished us. This love of God is demonstrated in our lives by our obedience to God's commands. Through this love, we will do the following:

- Obey all of God's commandments, and be true to him.
- Live a life of righteousness and truth, and submit to God.
- Keep ourselves pure from all sinful defilements of the flesh and spirit.
- Keep ourselves from the love of the world, which Apostle John says is not of the Father, and which James warns is enmity with God[49].
- Keep in constant communion with God through his Holy Spirit that indwells us.
- Resist the devil and his temptations.
- Resist all allurements of our flesh to lead us into sin.

- Pray without ceasing.
- Love one another and forgive one another as he commanded us.
- We should seek to keep all his commandments including faithfully preaching the gospel to all our world, paying our tithes, fasting and praying always, and being watchful lest the devil tempts us to sin.

In conclusion, let us ask and answer the question that Paul asked the Roman Christians in Romans 8:35, concerning the love of God:

> *Who shall separate us from the love of Christ? Shall tribulation, or distress, or persecution, or famine, or nakedness, or sword, or peril? As it is written, for thy sake we are killed all the day long; we are accounted as sheep for the slaughter. Nay in all these things we are more than conquerors through him that loved us. For I am persuaded that neither death, nor life, nor angels, nor principalities, nor powers, nor things present, nor things to come, nor height, nor depth, nor any other creature, shall be able to separate us from the love of God, which is in Christ Jesus our Lord.*

Let this be your constant confession and practice: That nothing shall ever separate you from abiding in God's love. Amen.

WORK BOOK

a) Define and explain "Love for God".
b) Do some people profess to know God, but in works deny him? (Titus 1:16). Can it happen to us too? Is there any area where this is happening in your own life?
c) In what 10 ways can you demonstrate your love for God?
d) Name some of the things that can threaten our love for God (Romans 8:35-39).
e) Summarize the message of this chapter in your own words

Practical Steps:

Resolve today that nothing shall ever separate you from the love of God. And remember that Love for God is obedience. Therefore you are saying that nothing shall ever deter you from obeying God.

LOVE ONE ANOTHER

*"By this shall all men know that ye are my disciples, if
ye have love one for another"* (John 13:35).

*"Jesus... having loved his own which were in the world,
he loved them unto the end"* (John 13:1).

Thought: It is far easier to love people from a distance. Once
they come close, we find faults.

Jesus was a great Lover, the greatest Lover that ever lived. No
one ever loved like him. He loves from the beginning to the
end. Just like God the Father who is described by John as Love,
even so Jesus Christ was Love personified when he walked on
earth, leaving us an example to follow his steps.

Jesus, the Greatest Lover

Jesus loved his disciples, and had great hope for every one of
them. He taught them, provided for them, cared for them, and
forgave their sins. Even at the end of his ministry when Judas
the betrayer came with the High Priest's soldiers to arrest him,
Jesus still called Judas, "Friend." He said, *"Friend, whence comest
thou?"* Even when Peter and all the disciples forsook him at his
arrest, Jesus still cared for them. He told the soldiers who came

to arrest him to allow the disciples to go, while he willingly surrendered himself. He even healed Malchus' ear (Malchus was a servant of the High Priest, whose ear Peter had cut off with a sword)... And despite Peter's denial of Jesus, the Lord still loved and forgave him.

Jesus washed his disciples' feet at the Last Supper to demonstrate his care and love for them. He lowered himself in love to serve his own. Jesus loved even his enemies. He taught us to love our enemies, to greet them, and do good things to those who hate us, and pray for those who despitefully use us and persecute us. He taught us to bless those who curse us, to bless and not to curse. We are also to lend to those who ask us, and to give generously to meet the needs of the poor and needy.

Jesus went about doing good things and healing the sick, and delivering all that were oppressed by the devil. He did this out of a heart of compassion, not for financial gain, and not to show off. He asked us to give freely of all that we have received freely from God.

A Ministry of Pure Love

Jesus' ministry on earth was all about love, caring, compassion, and mercy. He was love personified. Through his life and ministry we can understand that ministry is all about showing love to people, to all people, near and far away. He loved all, the good, the bad and the ugly. Although he hated wickedness and oppression, he held hope for erring sinners. He believed that they could repent and become children of God, and learn to do good things, and avoid evil.

Thus he forgave the woman who was caught red-handed in adultery. The Pharisees and their disciples wanted to stone her to death, but Jesus set her free... because at this time he came to save the world from sin, not to judge the world. He knew there is a coming day of judgment when sinners would burn like the oven; but today is a day to seek and save the lost. Thus even when he was in agonizing pains on the Cross of Calvary, he still prayed for his detractors and betrayers. He prayed and said, *"Lord, forgive them, for they know not what they do."*

No man ever loved like Jesus and he has left an indelible mark of perfect love for us to follow in his steps. Thus Apostle John, the apostle of love who lay his head on Jesus' shoulder at the last supper said, *"God is love and he that dwells in love dwells in God, and God in him... He that loveth not knoweth not God, for God is love"* (1 John 4:7-20).

Life Application

True Christianity is all about loving God and doing his commandments. Loving God passionately with all our heart, soul, and understanding, takes precedence. But the second great commandment is to love our neighbours as we love ourselves. In fact, the scriptures teach us that the person who claims to love God must prove his love by loving his neighbour. For if you cannot love your neighbour whom you are seeing around you, how can you claim to love God whom you have not seen?

From the examples and life of Christ, we can conclude that love of our neighbour is the true spirit of Christian life and ministry. And this love will embrace the following, and more:

I.   **Care for Poor Neighbours**
     Look out for your poor neighbours, relations and other poor folks, and help them in their distresses. Visit them in their infirmities and sicknesses, and offer valuable assistance to help them recover. The story of

the Good Samaritan told by Jesus shows that if we fail to show pity and compassionate care to those who suffer around us then we are as infidels before God. Similarly, the poor Lazaruses that languish within our reach (at our gates) must be helped, fed, clothed and given treatment[50]. Otherwise, we too may end up in hell for our wicked and uncompassionate hearts.

II. **Widows, Orphans, the Sick, Etc.**

True religion and undefiled before God and the Father is this, to visit the fatherless and the widows in their afflictions, and to keep oneself pure from the world[51]. Thus it is a good thing for each of us to embrace the ministry of outreach to these persons, including prisoners, the sick, the homeless, the naked, and the destitute. Ministration to these persons helps our hearts to be tender like the heart of Jesus. And we must do it with sincere hearts, not for public show or recognition.

III. **Forgiveness**

Forgiveness of those who sin or those who are against us is one of the high points of Christian love. Christ clearly showed us that if we fail to forgive others then our own sins will not be forgiven by God. No matter how grievous the sin, or how often it is committed, we are admonished to forgive and forget. Anyone who seriously considers himself or herself to be a disciple of Christ must take the matter seriously because Jesus emphasized greatly on this. Apostle Paul said that roots of bitterness and malice cause defilement among believers. And no defiled fellow will be allowed into God's presence. Forgiveness is our means of salvation, and we must extend same to others.

IV. Love Your Enemies

Love your enemies, and do good things to those who hate you[52]. This is one of the distinguishing traits of true Christianity. If we fail to do this then our profession of Christianity is not better than that of the heathen. This is what the Lord says. It will take the help of the Holy Spirit for you to love some people. But if you pray, God can shed his love in your heart, as he did for Stephen, who prayed to God for the forgiveness of the people who stoned him to death.

V. Pray for Others

Prayer for all those around you, and even for those that hate you, is one service that we all can freely give. It is obvious that from the standpoint of the New Testament, a lot of prayers that many Christians pray against their enemies are unscriptural. If anyone had any good reason to pray against their enemies, certainly Stephen, who was stoned to death by the unbelieving Jews, should have prayed against them: but instead he prayed that God should forgive them. Also Paul should have prayed against the Jews who sought to kill him, but rather he prayed for their salvation[53].

VI. Sharing the Word of God

Ministering the word of God to the ignorant and unbelievers is another way of demonstrating our love for the sinners around us. Why should we criticize the sinners if we have not endeavoured to shine the light of God's word into their lives?

VII. Eliminate Criticisms

We must learn to speak well of people, even those who may have offended us. Sometimes there is much uncharitable talk among Christian folk. We judge and criticize other children of God, and this exposes our unregenerate and uncharitable hearts. If we have nothing good to say about another child of God then let us please keep quiet, and pray for that saint. Do not allow your mouth to give vent to sarcastic remarks that can mar the reputation of that one for whom Christ died. And we should remember that for every idle word we speak we shall give account on the Day of Judgment[54].

VIII.   Forsake Wrath

Avoid anger, and forsake wrath. Even your righteous anger can become sin, if you fail to be sober and control your utterance. Moses' righteous anger against the murmuring of the people he was leading was explosive, and it caused him to disobey God's orders. Thus he was disallowed from entering the Promised Land[55]. Love is sober, kind, temperate and meek.

In conclusion, loving one another is one of the greatest traits and distinguishing marks of every true disciple of Christ. Like everyone else, it would be much easier for us to love fellow believers who do us good. But the true test of our Christian discipleship comes when we have to deal with believers who offend us; who offend God and are in sin; and when we have to deal with those who are our professed enemies and who seek our hurt. That is when the test of true Christian love should test strongly positive for us. Amen.

WORK BOOK

a) Mention one great proof that we are Jesus' disciples.

b) Give two reasons why we love people more from a distance. When they are closer we find faults because they are imperfect. But what about us? We have our own imperfections often hidden from us.

   If our love were perfected we would be able to accommodate the faults of others.

c) Mention at least four things that love would compel us to do for our enemies.

d) Name other ways we can express our love for other people. (Also read Matt 25:31-46).

e) What does God say we should do if our enemy is hungry, thirsty, or in some other need? (Rom 12:20-21).

f) Summarize the message of this chapter in your own words.

Practical Steps:

Go and do something today about your enemy that you know. Start by forgiving him. Then go the extra mile and do something good to him. Don't stop.

OBEDIENCE UNTO DEATH

Though he was a Son, yet learned he obedience by the things which he suffered (Hebrews 5:8).

For even hereunto were ye called: because Christ also suffered for us, leaving us an example, that ye should follow his steps: who knew no sin, neither was guile found in his mouth, (1 Peter 2:21-22).

Thought: When obedience involves suffering, be ready to go through it alone; not with the crowd.

One sure test of a true disciple of Christ is his willingness to stand up for his faith and to suffer if need be, for Christ. Christ had many admirers and would-be disciples who followed him. But when things got tough and rough, many of them deserted him, and others joined the crowd to shout, *"Crucify him, crucify him."*

Obedience to God is often very costly. Why? Because a whole lot of people in this world are not obedient to God, and your determination to obey him is contrary to all their way of life. They are used to living in disobedience; they are used to doing things their own way, and they do not want anybody telling them how to do things. Your trying to do things differently will make many people mad at you.

When Christ first announced his mission to Jerusalem to die for our sins, it was not only Peter who found it offensive. All the disciples felt it was not necessary; they felt it was not in line with the current nature of things. They were having a wonderful ministry with miracles, signs and wonders. People were being healed, Christ was being glorified, and they themselves were enjoying the limelight. It was as if Christ was trying to spoil their joy by talking about going to die at Jerusalem. That was why Peter spoke out the mind of everyone else, *"Be it far from thee, Lord: this shall not be unto thee."*

In fact after the Lord had spoken more on this, many of the other disciples (not the twelve) deserted him, and left... When you talk of suffering for your faith, or for the Lord, you will find people becoming uncomfortable, and some will start to leave. But obedience will often involve suffering, and you should be ready to suffer for your Lord. The Bible declares unequivocally that if we suffer with him then we shall reign with him. But if we deny him, he also will deny us (2 Timothy 2:12).

Life Application

Christianity would have been such an appealing and universal religion but for God's requirement of obedience to his commandments. And those commandments, though not grievous to the saints, are however grievous to the disobedient ones. You will be opposed by friends and neighbours when you try to be obedient to God's commands. (But that is how God really proves those who love him in truth). The world revels in pleasure, leisure, and things that please the flesh. It has its own codes of conduct and practices different from God's. And it demands conformity to community ways of doing things.

People will resist changes, especially if it will make them uncomfortable. And if you insist on being different you may be treated as an enemy or a renegade. People will gossip about you: your self-righteousness, your incorrigible nature, your non-conformist lifestyle, etc. Christ said that they will cast you out from their company. They will say you are difficult to get along with, and that you are antisocial or a religious bigot.

Then if you try to share the gospel with them, many will shun you, and turn around to persecute you. Of course, we all know that many ardent unyielding believers have met their untimely deaths at the hands of religious or secular bigots who oppose the Christian faith in their societies and nations. From Jerusalem to Rome to the ends of the earth the gospel message has been carried often by rivers of blood of saints who had to give up their lives for the gospel they so much cherished and embraced.

Obedience is Costly

Today as ever before God demands total obedience from each one of us his children. Obedience to the word of God, or to his revelation, or to an errand he sends us can earn us being thrown into the fire or into the den of lions. It earned John the Baptist a beheaded head, and death to all the apostles, except probably John. Whatever it may be, obedience is required from each one of us, and it can be very costly. You may lose a job, lose money, lose your freedom, be incarcerated, be maligned, suffer in many other ways, lose friends, etc.

It is even possible to lose one's life striving to obey God. But if we obey God, the end is bound to be glorious, either now or much later in God's kingdom. But if we deny God and disobey him, or compromise with the world, the end will be bitter. Come what may, God has promised that he will never leave us, nor forsake us. And Christ says that all power in heaven and on earth has been given unto him, and he enjoins us to go in that understanding. He will be with us even to the end of the world (Matthew 28:18).

Whatever we encounter in our pilgrimage as believers in this temporal world, we can be sure of this truth: God will never forsake his people. And he is able to save to the uttermost those who place their faith in him. He is the Rock of Ages, a hiding place in the storms of life, and the mighty Deliverer of Israel. He is the Lord that never fails. His power and understanding is infinite, and his eyes run to and fro throughout the whole earth to show his awesome strength on behalf of those who put their trust in him [56]. *"So that we may boldly say, The Lord is my Helper, and I will not fear what man shall do unto me"* (Hebrews 13:6).

WORK BOOK

a) Did Christ suffer in obeying God? If yes, why are we unwilling to suffer likewise?

b) "When obedience involves suffering, many friends will desert you." Discuss with any examples.

c) Discuss any occasion when you refused to join the multitude to do evil. What followed?

d) Name some New Testament martyrs and others in contemporary times. What happened?

e) Why does God often allow us to go through suffering, when he has the power to deliver us?

f) Why does God often test our obedience? What happened when Abraham obeyed God in the matter of sacrificing Isaac?

g) Summarize the message of this chapter in your own words.

Practical steps:

Which areas of life have you found it so difficult to fully obey God? Can you now pray for grace to obey him completely? Go ahead and obey God, and reap the blessing sooner or later.

ATTRIBUTES OF CHRIST (11)

ZEAL FOR GOD

"The zeal of thine house hath consumed me" (John 2:17).

"And he (Jehu) said, Come with me and see my zeal for the Lord…" (2 Kings 10:16).

Thought: "Much good, much enlargement, and much progress would have been wrought for the kingdom of God if professors of Christian religion did their work with greater zeal and passion."

Christ was meek and gentle, longsuffering and full of kindness and love, but when he saw his Father's house being turned into a market-place by money merchants he could not take it kindly. That was what happened at the Passover Feast in Jerusalem. Christ was really angry at this unholy breach of conduct, this show of irreverence towards God's holy temple. And immediately he made a scourge of small cords, and used them to whip them all out of the temple, including the sheep, cattle, and doves. *"He poured out the money changers' money, and overthrew the tables"* (v.15). Some people must have lost quite some money that day!

Also in the days of Moses, God's wrath was kindled against Israel because they were committing fornication with the

77

daughters of the people of Moab and eating their idolatrous sacrifices. And while the elders were mourning because of God's anger and plague on Israel, a male Israelite, Zimri, brought a Midianite lady, Cozbi, into the camp for a sex frenzy. But Phinehas, the son of Aaron took a javelin and went after them in the tent, and slew them... And this was written as a memorial and honour for Phinehas, and God promised him the privilege of a perpetual priesthood in Israel *"because he was zealous for his God"* (Numbers 25:13).

Life Application

When it comes to the things of God we find that many saints are lacking in zeal. It is as if the work of God is not urgent, and not so important. We do God's work when it is convenient, when we are less busy, when all other "more important" work has been done. This was the complaint of Apostle Paul to the Philippian church, *"For all seek their own, not the things which are Jesus Christ's"* (Philippians 2:21).

But it was not so with the Lord Jesus. For him the Lord's work took priority over every other work. He told his parents who were looking for him after one of the Passover Feasts, when he was 12 years old, *"How is it that ye sought me? Wist ye not that I must be about my Father's business?"* For Christ, the Father's business was overriding. In fact, scriptures record that at times he was so engrossed in ministry that there was no time to eat food[57]. So his friends sought to come and take him away by force.

Work with Passion

Friends, let us put more passion into God's work. As has been said by some wise folks, God's work is eternal but we do not have eternity to do it. We only have a brief sojourn here on earth, and while we tarry, and engage in other "more lucrative" and temporal work, many souls die, and others escape our reach. And we miss much valuable opportunity. There are also some who would have built an empire or a conglomerate for Christ if they had applied more passion and vision for the things of God. But because they lacked these things they ended up wasting their abundant resources on perishable commodities and pleasure trips, and things of no enduring value to the kingdom of God.

God through Jeremiah, placed a curse on those who do God's work deceitfully, or negligently. And in Amos he said, *"Woe to those who are at ease in Zion, who sleep on ivory beds, and eat lamb's meat, and are unconcerned with the travails of Jacob".*

It is time for us to embrace the zeal of Christ in all our labours for the Lord. Let us be zealous in preaching the gospel, in visitations to church members who are not showing up, in praying for fellow church members and pastors, in follow-up, in conducting Bible studies, in church-planting, in witnessing for Christ, in printing more Bibles, etc. The gospel can only cover much ground if we all brace up, and put in more effort and more time to do our Father's business. If we neglect the work, the kingdom of God suffers.

However, if we arise, like Nehemiah, we can together rebuild the broken walls of our Jerusalem and God will be glorified through our labours. One thing is sure, any way: God will honour those who labour for him. And he will give his eternal rewards to each one of us according to how we have travailed for him.

"And, behold I come quickly; and my reward is with me, to give every man according as his work shall be" (Revelation 22:12).

WORK BOOK

a) How zealous are you for the Lord? How have you proved your zeal?

b) When unbelievers make fun of the Lord and of the church, do you just remain mute? Do you use wisdom to put in a positive word for the Lord? Do you make a public stand for him?

c) What ministry are you engaged in for the Lord, and how much have you proven yourself in it?

d) How much time do you give to do the Lord's work each week? Or, are you just a church-goer?

e) Summarize the message of this chapter in your own words.

Practical steps:

Prayerfully determine a ministry where God would have you engage in. And start doing something fulfilling for God.

ATTRIBUTES OF CHRIST (12)

MAN OF VISION

Jesus... for the joy that was set before him endured the cross, despising the shame, and is set down at the right hand of God (Hebrews 12:2).

For he (Abraham) looked for a city which hath foundations, whose builder and maker is God ...not having received the promises, but having seen them afar off...(Hebrews 11:10, 13)

Thought: As the northern star to the ship, so is vision to the soul.

The Lord Jesus was a man of vision. He saw far ahead of time what was destined for him, what God had prepared for him after his earthly travails. For him it was not a dim vision, it was not a clouded probability: it was a glorious reality which present distresses could not becloud!

Jesus saw beyond his earthly sojourn. He saw beyond his temptations and trials. He saw beyond the temporal gains offered by Satan; he saw beyond the betrayals of Judas, his abandonment by his close disciples, and Peter's denials. Christ saw beyond the scathing abuses and the pains and the shame

81

and suffering at the cross. He did not allow his mind to dwell on these immediate circumstances.

He looked into the future, the events after the cross: he saw himself in the resurrection, ascending to the Father, and seated at his right hand; all power and authority given to him, and all principalities and powers made subject to him. He saw the fruit of his travails: sons of God reconciled to God by his shed blood. He saw millions, and probably even billions of sons of God, reigning in glory through his sacrifice and suffering. And he was satisfied. Therefore he despised the cross, the pain, and the shame. And today he is set at the right hand of God. Alleluia!

What if Christ had focused on the immediate; the pains, the shame, the jeering crowd, the agony? He probably would have called for more than twelve legions of angels from the Father to deliver him. And the result would have been aborting the process of our salvation, the joy of heaven would have been taken away, and the exceeding glory of his name would never have been. But thanks be to God that Christ set his mind on that joyous and excellent glory that was prepared for him, and so he endured the cross, despising the pain and the shame.

Life Application

For each of us who would be disciples of Christ, there is a cross to carry; there are seasons of shame and pain; there are rivers to cross and mountains to climb on our pilgrimage to the holy Land. If we focus on those temporal setbacks or travails we could be tempted to stop, or to turn back. There may be dark clouds that the jet-plane must penetrate, but the pilot, following the radar knows that there is no turning back. For beyond those foreboding clouds there is a place called home: a place of joy, and family. So the pilot steps on the 'throttle' without looking back.

- No pain, no gain
- No cross, no crown
- No risk, no worthwhile result

This is what will keep you going in spite of all odds; indeed, vision sees beyond the present! It counts all things loss for the prize of the high calling of God. Vision has counted the cost, and knows that the end is far more glorious than the present. For the man of vision, there is no turning back.

The preacher said, *"He that observeth the wind shall not sow; and he that regardeth the clouds shall not reap."*[58] Therefore, sow into your vision, regardless of opposition, regardless of your lack. The vision will grow if you sow into it with the wisdom of God; but if you do not sow, it will die. And reap your vision regardless of constraints here and there, for if you do not reap the harvest, it will spoil.

Your vision will propel you to investments, goals, projects:

1. Invest your time. The vision will become clearer if you give it enough time.
2. Invest your money. Do not be diverted to other things. Invest your money directly into developing the vision, and make it self-sustaining.
3. Invest in men that will help you run with the vision. Invest in teachings, trainings, equipping them. Multiply yourself.
4. Invest in prayers, and get helpers to pray with you.
5. Market the vision, it will attract investors.
6. Consolidate. Then expand the vision. Then consolidate again and expand.
7. Get good counsel. Keep running with the vision, and do not allow any setbacks to stop you.

The vision will surely speak in the end, and you will ever be glad you ran with it. When everything else fails, your vision will sustain you. *"Without a vision the people perish."*

Remember, the vision is not just making heaven (as great as that would be). It is making it with flying colours and accolades, all by grace!! Therefore go to God now, wait on him, and catch a vision for your life. Lives are wasted without a vision.

WORK BOOK

a) What is vision?

b) What helped the Lord Jesus to endure the shame and pain of the cross? What did he see?

c) What is your own vision for your life and for God?

d) Is there any worthy vision without difficulties? What will happen if you focus on the immediate difficulties?

e) Enumerate the investments you must make to push your vision. Explain why each is necessary.

f) A vision from God will most likely look bigger than you can carry, but through prayer and the help of God you can actualize it. What are the other features of a vision from God?

g) Summarize the message of this chapter in your own words.

Practical steps:

Go to God and catch a vision for your life, something that God requires you to do for him: it could be in the church, or for a fellowship, or in your family, or in the business place, or for a set of people, or for charity, etc.

THE DIVINE PRESENCE

...Ye shall be scattered, every man to his own, and shall leave me alone: and yet I am not alone, because the Father is with me... He that sent me is with me (John 16:32; 8:29).

And the whole multitude sought to touch him: for there went virtue out of him, and healed them all (Luke 6:19).

Thought: When Moses came down from the mountain he did not know that his face was shining. The secret is in the mountain.

There is nothing more comforting, nothing more reassuring than to know that the Greater One is with you, and in you. Jesus had this knowledge, and lived in close fellowship and communion with the indwelling Father. God spoke constantly to him, and sometimes audibly too. For Jesus, God was not just in heaven, but God was with him and in him, and working through him to reach the world; "The Father was in Christ reconciling the world to himself"[59]. It was an intimate relationship. God was closer to Christ than any friend could be, for he was in him. For this reason Christ could not be intimidated by circumstances, or by men, or by Satan. He said,

"The Father that sent me is with me, for I do always that which is pleasing to him."

Other men of God who excelled with God also had such knowledge of God's abiding presence. They could literally "feel" his presence: Paul said, *"At my first answer no man stood with me, but all men forsook me… nevertheless the Lord stood with me and strengthened me…"* (2 Timothy 4:16-17). Elijah said, *"As the Lord liveth, before whom I stand…"* David said, *"Thou knowest my down sitting and my uprising; thou understands my thoughts afar off. Thou compassest my path and my lying down… whither shall I go from thy spirit, or whither shall I flee from thy presence? …When I awake I am still with thee"* (Psalm 139). Jeremiah said, "But the Lord is with me as a mighty terrible one" (Jeremiah 20:11). Job said, *"Now my eye seeth thee."*

You are God's Abode

God himself said concerning us, *"I will dwell in them, and walk in them; and they shall be my people, and I shall be their God"*[60]. Paul said, *"Know ye not that ye are the temple of God, and that the Spirit of God dwells in you?"* Christ said, *"He that keepeth my word is he that loveth me, and my Father will love him; and we shall come and make our abode in him"* (John 14:21,23). He further said, *"Behold I stand at the door and knock: if any man hear my voice and open the door, I will come in to him, and will sup with him, and he with me"* (Revelation 3:20).

In his darkest hours Jesus was comforted by the divine Presence. It was only when that Presence lifted at the cross that he was troubled and cried out to God. And that Presence was lifted because of the burden of our sins which he took upon himself. The divine Presence in him wrought miracles among the people. Virtue flowed from him and healed the people, the divine Presence in him also repelled and cast out demons.

The divine Presence gave him victory over demons, Satan, and hell. The return of the divine Presence wrought the miracle of his resurrection from the dead. Are you flowing in the divine Presence? How can we also command the divine Presence, since he has promised that he will not leave us comfortless, and that he will send his Spirit to dwell with us forever?

Life Application

When we invite Jesus into our lives as our Lord and Saviour, or when we are baptized into the Holy Spirit, the Lord comes to dwell in us, to be our Friend, to be our Counsellor, to teach and guide and empower us, and to be our divine Helper. He comes in to interact with us, to enjoy fellowship with us, to commune (discuss) with us, and to bless us and make us an instrument of blessing for our family, church, community and nation.

The Neglect of God

But very often we do not allow him to fulfil these functions. We do not even treat him as a Person, but as an "it." We neglect him, dump him in the back seat of our cars, and zoom off! Day after day, week after week, and for months and years many Christians talk, act, and live without communing with the Holy Spirit. We render him inoperative, keep him incommunicado, and as it were, we frustrate his visit. He is like an unwanted Visitor, locked up in one of our closets, while we take charge of our affairs, very rarely recognizing his Presence, very rarely asking for his counsel, and hardly fellowshipping with him. When we get into trouble, or when we lose our way, it is then we remember that we have an all-powerful Holy Spirit who is supposed to be with us till the end of the world. No wonder many times we do not get all the help we need: because the Holy Spirit feels neglected, quenched, and not needed.

Cultivate His Presence

But if only we can now recognize his continued abiding Presence; if only we will have more fellowship with him as a Person living in his own temple, which is our body, our spirit; if only we will talk with him daily and often, and call him *"Sweet Holy Spirit"*, and thank him for leading us, and seek his counsel, and acknowledge his wisdom, power, and love in our lives... If only we would cultivate more friendship and interaction with him, he will do wonders in our midst. He will show himself more and more, teach us divine counsel, do miracles with us, empower us in ministry, and speak through us, and do the mighty works of God through us and with us. He would reveal Jesus to us, and through us, as promised.

Our presence, or rather his presence in us, will repel demons, cast out devils, heal the sick, and do many wonderful things that would glorify God. Then we would do the works of Christ, and greater works.

Friends, let us cultivate the presence of Christ, let us practise being in his presence, more often. Let us affirm his presence using the promises in the Word of God, and meditate on his presence. Let us visualize him with us, and let us speak to him, and listen and hear in our spirit-man what he would answer us. If we create enough time to be in his presence and to commune with him, then, very soon his presence will be with us everywhere we are, and his virtue and power will flow through us into our world to meet the needs of the world around us.

WORK BOOK

a) What do you understand by "The Divine Presence?"

b) Name some secrets of attaining to the Divine Presence.

c) If God is in heaven, how can he be with men on earth? Read 2 Corinthians 6:16.

d) Practice makes perfect. Have you ever practised the presence of God? What was the result?

e) If you really knew that God indwelt you moment by moment, how would that affect your life, attitude, behaviour, etc.?

f) Explain the communion of the Holy Spirit.

g) Summarize the message of this chapter in your own words.

Practical step:

1) Practise the divine Presence this week.

2) Commune with the Holy Spirit today and all through this week.

BOLDNESS

Now when they saw the boldness of Peter and John, and perceived that they were unlearned and ignorant men, they marvelled; and they took knowledge of them, that they had been with Jesus (Acts 4:13).

And now Lord behold their threatening: and grant unto thy servants that with all boldness they may speak thy word (Acts 4:29).

Thought: The man had great capabilities, and would have done great things; but, alas, he was incapacitated by fear.

When God gives a man a task to perform, and especially when that task will meet the displeasure or disapproval of men, then that man must muster courage or boldness to do it, otherwise that job will never get done. The assignment that God gave Christ to accomplish on earth was one such assignment. He was sent on a mission to kings, princes, governors, ecclesiastical personalities, leaders of the people, and the common people. His mission was to warn, correct, rebuke and teach people. He was sent to expose the wickedness and evil doings of the people, to warn them of the consequences of their ways, to preach righteousness and truth, and establish God's way in the nation, preparing men and women for the coming kingdom of God.

Can you imagine going to tell the king to his face that he was committing adultery, by marrying a woman whose husband was still alive? That is what someone like John the Baptist did! Can you imagine telling a governor that another government is coming to displace his government? That was Christ's mission! Can you tell the High Priest that he is a sinner?

The task before Christ was an enormous task. It required the soul of a lion to deliver his message. John the Baptist had been killed for daring to say such things. If Christ was to deliver his message he should make up his mind to be willing to die. But alas, his mind was already made up from the beginning. He was ready to die, if need be, to fulfil his mission. And that was what gave him great boldness. Throughout the Scriptures, and to this present day, all men who have ever accomplished any worthwhile goals for God have been men of extraordinary courage.

They were ready to die for what they believed in. They counted the message that they carried to be far greater than their own lives.

On his last journey to Jerusalem, the Bible records that there was fear on all sides. The disciples were afraid. But Jesus, like a general that he was, went ahead of them, boldly with his head lifted. Come what may, he had been preparing for this hour, and he would face it without fear or trembling, but with boldness.

Life Application

What assignment has God given you to do for him in your days, and for your generation? Surely God must have an assignment for you if indeed you are a son or daughter of the King of kings. Find out his will for your life. It could be he is sending you to governors or government officials to warn them about corruption in the nation, or to tell them the simple message of Christ, and to warn them to repent from sin. It could be he is sending you to students in the universities, or to church leaders and pastors. It could be some other assignment.

It may seem formidable, too huge to perform. You may feel incapable, ill-equipped, unqualified. Yes, but if God has laid the matter in your heart, it could be that he has searched for someone and found you the most suitable person for his use. Do not ask him to send someone else, as some people do, and as Moses did. Ask him for the boldness you need to get the task done. And if you get that task done, he could change your name to "Moses" – the Moses of your generation.

God does not usually use the "high and mighty" to accomplish his tasks. He uses the despised things of this world, the weak, and the "ignorant and unlearned" men to raise the dead, and cast out demons, and do great works. If he could use Jeremiah who said "I cannot speak, for I am but a child", then he can use you. And remember he warned Jeremiah not to go with that "I can't" mind-set, and not to fear the people, otherwise he (God) would confound Jeremiah before them[61]! If God could use young David, bypassing the high and mighty warriors in the camp of Israel, then he can also use you.

Pray for More Boldness

Pray for more boldness. That assignment will not take off if you do not muster courage.

The Lord's business requires haste, and if you tarry, the assignment can be given to others who may be less qualified than you, but who are willing to go with boldness, with faith in God. Paul regularly prayed for boldness (Ephesians 6:19;

Philippians 1:20). He asked the brethren to pray for him so that he would deliver his message with boldness, and enter doors that God had opened, with boldness. And his boldness caused many to believe in Jesus, and caused miracles to follow his message.

- Christ spoke and acted boldly[62]
- His apostles ministered with boldness[63]
- Paul was bold[64]
- Barnabas waxed bold[65]
- Apollos spoke boldly[66]
- Indeed, the righteous are bold like lions[67]

You too should wax bold and be strong. Pray for the spirit of boldness. You need it to do the work of God!

Let everyone whom God has called, and given a work to do for the kingdom of God, do such works with the spirit of boldness. That was Christ's way of doing things. He would respect men, but he would not allow the fear of men to stand between him and his God-given assignment. And this boldness of Christ rubbed off mightily on his disciples. They spoke with boldness and acted with boldness. Yes, and so must we!

WORK BOOK

a) Define "Boldness". How does it come? (Ephesians 6:19; Philippians 1:20)
b) Why do we need it? What happens when we do God's work with fear of men?
c) Explain 2 Timothy 1:7.
d) What great opportunities have you missed in life because of fear?

e) Why are many brethren unwilling to minister or witness for Christ? Is it not due to fear? Suddenly the mouth becomes heavy, and the person is tongue-tied: is it not fear of men? What does the Bible say about the fear of men? (Proverbs 29:25).

f) Can the fearful and faint-hearted do any great works for the Lord? (The fearful hide their talents). In Matthew 25:25, the unfruitful servant was afraid. Discuss.

g) Summarize the message of this chapter in your own words.

Practical steps:

Which of your talents have you hidden because of fear? Dig it up today, and start using it.

ATTRIBUTES OF CHRIST (15)

THE WORD OF GOD

In the beginning was the Word, and the Word was with God, and the Word was God. The same was in the beginning with God (John 1:1-2).

He sent his word, and healed them, and delivered them from their destructions (Psalm 107:20).

Thought: God created the world with spoken words. Christ healed the sick, raised the dead, and stilled storms with words. We too should operate with words, as sons of God.

The Lord Jesus operated his ministry by prayers and by outreach with power-packed words. Through prayer God showed him the day's assignment, and what he was to do. Then as he went forth to minister, teach, heal and preach, he did all these with the words of his mouth. His words carried fire-power! Those who heard him said, *"What a word is this! For with authority and power commandeth he even the unclean spirits, and they come out"* (Luke 4:36).

Jesus was the embodiment of the will and word of God. He said he did not come to speak his own words, but the words of he that sent him. So as he spoke, God honoured his words because Christ did not seek his own glory, but only the glory of God. He sought to do only those things that were pleasing to God. Jesus knew the word of God because he had breathed those words from the beginning. Scriptures declare that the holy men of God (the prophets) spoke as they were inspired by the Holy Ghost. Even the scribes wondered at him, *"How knoweth this man letters, having never learned?"*

Jesus knew the power of God's words. He told the disciples not to worry about his departure to the Father, but that they should operate with his words. He said, *"The flesh profits nothing"* (i.e. my physical presence with you is not that important) – *"The words I have spoken to you, they are spirit and they are life."* If they used his words, spoke his words, walked in his words, obeyed his words, and taught his words; then all things would be possible to them. *"Whosoever shall say to this mountain, be lifted up, and be thou cast into the sea; and shall not doubt in his heart, but believe that those things which he saith shall come to pass; he shall have whatsoever he saith"* (Mark 11:22-24).

But he emphasized that his disciples should keep his words, because those who keep his words are those who love him, and he and the Father would manifest their glory to such a one[68]. Further, he said that if his words dwell in us, and we dwell in him, then whatsoever we ask shall be done for us. This was the basis of Christ's astounding ministry, and the basis of his miracles: he was filled with the word of God, not his own words. He spoke only what the Father told him to speak. He obeyed the word of God fully. He spoke the word of God with power and authority to situations, circumstances, demons, and men. And as he spoke, the Holy Spirit moved with the word to accomplish great things for God and his work on earth.

Life Application

If Jesus' ministry was based on prayer and spoken words, then we should pattern our lives and ministry likewise. We must pray on each occasion to know beforehand what we may encounter in the day and how to handle it. We must ask God, as occasion demands, what we must do in every situation, and what we must say. Let us study the word of God and know it. The actual word of God we possess is the one we have etched in our memory and spirit through memorization, affirmation, meditation and confession. The word of God that is only in the Bible, but not in our hearts, is not really with us. It is mere letters until we know that word, accept it, obey it, internalize it, and use it.

Be Filled with God's Word

The scriptures enjoin us to be filled with the word in all wisdom and spiritual understanding. Meditate upon it night and day as God told Joshua, and it will make your way prosperous, and grant you good success. Commune with God based on his word. Speak this word with faith. The word of God that you confess with your mouth, and believe in your heart will bring you salvation and righteousness. The word of God in your heart will keep you from sin [69].

Speak the word boldly, with faith, and miracles will follow, doors will open to you, demons will flee, and God's work in your life will move forward. The spoken word of God will change your ministry forever. Be filled with the word, for out of the abundance of the heart the mouth speaketh. Above all, obey the word, and act on it. Your life will never be the same. *"Through faith we understand that the worlds were framed by the word of God, so that the things which are seen were not made of things which do appear"* (Hebrews 11:3).

Your most powerful tool is not necessarily how hard you work, though hard work is important. Your most productive tool is your faith-filled word, operated in the power of the Holy Spirit, and in accordance with the will of God. Through your word you can create your world.

WORK BOOK

a) Christ operated his ministry by prayers and the use of faith-filled words. Explain.

b) Is it possible for us to speak only the words of God? How?

c) Have you read through the entire Bible? How many times have you read through the entire Bible?

d) Enumerate some benefits in reading through the Bible?

e) What is the value of knowing God's will without obeying it?

f) What things and circumstances should you address with the word of God?

g) Summarize the message of this chapter in your own words.

Practical steps:

Start a programme of completing the reading of the entire Bible once each year. You can use a daily devotional to do that.

EARNEST FERVENT PRAYERS

"And being in agony he prayed more earnestly; and his sweat was as it were great drops of blood falling down to the ground" (Luke 22:44).

"The earnest fervent prayer of a righteous man availeth much" (James 5:16b).

Thought: Too busy to pray; too busy to receive divine help.

The Lord Jesus prayed more than most men of his day. Though he was the Son of God, born of the Holy Ghost, living a holy and sinless life… yet he found it needful to pray, and to pray more often, and more earnestly than most men ever prayed. While the disciples yet slept he woke early before dawn and went to a secluded place to pray. At the onset of his three and half year ministry, he took a long 40-day prayer–fast, eating nothing. Sometimes he went to the mountain all alone, and prayed all night. Then at the conclusion of his ministry, just before his suffering and crucifixion, he went to Beth-phage, and at the garden of Gethsemane he prayed the most vigorous prayer ever prayed by man. *"Being in agony he prayed more earnestly; and his sweat was as it were great drops of blood falling down to the ground."*

What do we learn from all these recorded prayer sessions and the prayer-life of the Lord? Why should he have laboured so much in prayers, though the Son of God, though blameless and holy? We may not understand fully why it had to be so, but at least we know that a great deal was at stake, especially at the cross: the burden of the salvation of all mankind was on his shoulders, and he still had a choice to accept the agonizing suffering at the cross, or to reject it, and call for legions of angels to dismiss Satan and his murderous crowd. He knew that of his own self he could do nothing.

He needed the power of God to sustain him, and help him continue to do what he knew was best. At that moment the full weight of our eternity rested on him. He needed heaven to intervene, and he prayed until God sent an angel to encourage him.

Life Application

Whenever holy men of God prayed intensely, especially often with fasting, God has been moved to do extraordinary things that would not normally be done. Through earnest fervent prayers of Elijah, heaven was locked, so that it did not rain for three and half years. Then when he prayed again, heaven gave rain.

Daniel, Nehemiah, Hannah, Cornelius the Centurion, and many others received miraculous answers to prayer.

The Jerusalem church was aghast when Herod took Apostle James, and killed him. But when he also took Peter and imprisoned him, waiting till after the Passover feast to kill him also, then the whole church woke up to earnest fervent prayers without ceasing. God answered them, Peter was released, and Herod was slain by worms. Glory!

Fervent Prayers Work Wonders

Friends, what do we learn from all these?

1. God intervenes in human affairs as men pray and seek his help. As long as we are comfortable with the situation, and feel we can handle things by ourselves, or that our friends can help us, God will wait for us to handle it by ourselves.

2. There is no difficulty, trouble, temptation, or Satan's armour that God cannot deal with. All things are possible with God, depending on whether or not we seek him.

3. Depending on the matter at stake, we may need to engage in seasons of fasting, along with our prayers.

4. It is good many times to engage the assistance of fellow saints in seeking God's help. Christ certainly beckoned on his disciples to assist him at Gethsemane. And Paul often requested the churches to pray for him.

5. Your prayer life will determine the level of victory you attain in all affairs of your life and ministry.

6. Holy living, faith, and your prayers will determine the outcome of many issues of your life.

7. If the Lord Jesus could pray the way he did, then we ought to pray the more, because unlike him, we are beset with many shortcomings.

8. If we do not pray, we are telling God to hands off since we can handle the matter by ourselves.

9. The Lord said that there are matters that cannot be resolved except through fasting and prayers[70].

10. Holy living, deliverance from temptations, working of miracles, divine provisions, breakthroughs, good success, gifts of the Spirit, wisdom, wealth, good

health, long life, healings, and every other thing we need comes to us from God only as we seek him in prayers. Therefore we cannot afford to play with our prayer-life.

No Compromise with Prayers

You can pray three times a day like Daniel[71]. Though a very busy man, next to the king in the kingdom of Babylon, yet, Daniel prayed three times every day. Even when a satanic decree was issued that no man should pray to any man or God for thirty days, Daniel persisted in his prayers. He was not afraid of the king's decree, and the death sentence that accompanied it for offenders. He knew he could not live without communion with God. He knew his life and sustenance and power depended on constant communion with God. So he refused to obey that decree or compromise. And though he was eventually thrown into the den of lions, yet his God whom he trusted saved him.

Do not compromise your prayer life, because your life's essence depends on your communion and fellowship with God. Prioritize your life, do not clutter your life with activities, cut off all unnecessary items, and make sure you devote at least one to two hours daily for prayer and meditation. In this way God will soon honour you, because he honours those who honour him[72]. And he promises that those who seek him early will find him[73]. Amen.

WORK BOOK

a) Christ Jesus, though the Son of God, prayed more earnestly and more often than most men of his day. Discuss why?

b) Have you ever prayed with sweating? With bleeding? What do we learn from this?

c) Name some men who prayed seriously in the Scriptures, and the results of their prayers.

d) After the death of James, what saved Peter? What does this teach us about corporate intense prayers?

e) If you do not pray, what signals does it send to God?

f) Enumerate 7 lessons we learn from the teaching on prayers.

g) Summarize the message of this chapter in your own words.

Practical steps:

Trim off your excess activities and baggage. Resolve from today to pray three times daily; a total of at least one to two hours, or more.

THE FEAR OF GOD

It is a fearful thing to fall into the hands of the living God (Hebrews 10:31).

Christ... in the days of his flesh, when he had offered up prayers and supplications with strong crying and tears unto him that was able to save him from death, and was heard in that he feared, though he were a Son, yet learned he obedience by the things which he suffered (Hebrews 5:7-8).

Thought: "Fools rush in where angels fear to tread" -Alexander Pope.

It is true that we sometimes act presumptuously, and often take things for granted, until we are hurt. Some people will not stop meddling with some matters until they are disciplined, and familiarity often breeds contempt. But in the case of our Lord Jesus Christ, he never took his Father-God for granted.

He knew that in order to maintain a lawful universe and even a beautiful Paradise in a perfect state, the same God of unspeakable love is also the God of judgment, and law and order. Therefore, he feared God and was subject to him, though he was the only begotten Son of God's bosom. Christ obeyed

God because he loved him, but also because he feared him. The Psalmist said, *"Thou, even thou art to be feared: and who may stand in thy sight when once thou art angry?"*

Even Moses experienced this aspect of God's fear when he spent forty days and nights tarrying before God because of the sin of Israel. He said, *"I was afraid of the anger and hot displeasure of the Lord wherewith he was wroth against you to destroy you"* (Deuteronomy 9:10).

Of course there are many other reasons to fear the LORD. He is to be held in holy awe and reverence because of his great glory, power, majesty, and holiness. He is the Almighty, the awesome God, the Creator of our lives, who also created and sustains the entire universe.

Then when we consider our very salvation, and how through his love, he did not spare his only Son, but gave him freely to die for our sins, we must stand in continual reverence of such an Almighty God!

Life Application

If Jesus, the holy and unblemished Son of God, could give God reverence and fear, then what about us? If we forget to fear God we could fall into sin or error. And, if we do not repent soon enough, then in order for God to bring us out of our mess, he is sure to chasten us like any loving father would.

And we know that the Bible is true when it says, *"No chastening for the moment seemeth joyous, but afterwards it yieldeth the peaceable fruit of righteousness to those who are exercised thereby."* As the psalmist said, *"It is good for me that I have been afflicted, that I might learn thy statutes"* (Psalm 119:71). Thus the fear of God keeps us from sin, which is why the scriptures also declared that the fear of God is the beginning of wisdom[75].

We must all learn to imbibe the fear of the Lord because it is clean, converting the soul[76]. This fear of the Lord will manifest in different ways in our lives:

1. We will not toy with sin. In fact we will not tolerate circumstances or situations that may lead us into temptation. For example, close companionship or friendship with members of the opposite sex who are not our spouses can give room for indiscreet acts or infidelity. A man or woman who fears the Lord will be careful in such matters.

2. Watching sex movies on TV or the Internet, or pornographic materials, would lead us into temptation. We would not indulge in such things in order to keep our bodies and minds pure for the indwelling Holy Spirit.

3. We would fear to criticize, speak evil of, or judge other people, especially the brethren, because God has said that we should not do so. He alone is the Judge.

4. A man who fears the Lord will be kept from many evils, by his fear of the Lord. Thus he will do everything possible to keep his or her marriage intact, to run his or her business on Christian principles, pay tithes, pay taxes, pay his workers well, be careful of relationships with worldly people, fear and love the ministers of the gospel, bring up his or her children in the admonition of the Lord, etc.

May we all embrace the fear of the Lord because it is healthy for us! The following Scripture references tell us more about the fear of God:

*   *"Let the fear of the Lord be upon you[74]"*
*   *"The fear of the Lord is wisdom[75]"*

- *"The fear of the Lord is clean, enduring forever...*[76]*"*
- *"The fear of the Lord is to hate evil*[77]*"*
- *"The fear of the Lord prolongs days*[78]*"*
- *"The fear of the Lord is a fountain of life*[79]*"*
- *"Fear God and keep his commandments*[80]*"*
- *"Fear him who is able to destroy both soul and body in hell*[81]*"*
- *"Praise God, ye that fear him*[82]*"*
- *"Fear God and give glory to him*[83]*"*

"He that feareth him is accepted[84]*"*

WORK BOOK

a) *"It is a fearful thing to fall into the hands of the living God"* (Hebrews 10:31). Explain.

b) Why did Christ pray "with strong crying and tears"? What does this tell us about prevailing prayers?

c) Describe some of the attributes of God that make Him worthy of our fear.

d) What are some of the benefits of the fear of God?

e) How does Scripture describe "the fear of God"?

f) Summarize the message of this chapter in your own words.

Practical steps:

Our God is a consuming fire. If you have been indulging in some secret sin, be sure your sin will soon find you out. This is the time to quit; otherwise God may cast you into a bed of affliction (Revelation. 2:22).

FILLED WITH WISDOM AND GRACE

"Be ye therefore wise as serpents..." (Matthew 10:16).

"Great men are not always wise" (Job 32:9).

Thought: Wisdom does not merely know what to do. It also knows how to do it, when to do it, and then actually does it.

Christ grew in stature and wisdom and grace. Some men, even Christian men, only grow in stature, but with little wisdom. That is why many fall, because God sustains his own with wisdom. And he says if we lack wisdom, we should ask of God who gives wisdom liberally without upbraiding us for asking.

Wisdom entails knowing the times and seasons. There is a time to keep silence, and a time to speak up; there is a time to sow and another time to reap. You do not sow and reap at once... You will need to exercise a little patience, and then you will reap if you faint not.

Wisdom often depends on timing: Jesus knew when to speak up, and when to keep quiet. When the Jews came with stones to stone the woman taken in adultery, Jesus knew it was not time for arguments. Otherwise, they would have left the woman and stoned Jesus first. He used wisdom to dispel the crowd.

Wisdom is discerning. When the Herodians brought tribute money to entangle him, and pitch him against the Roman power, he discerned their intentions, and answered them with wisdom.

Then they went back to those who sent them, and testified, *"No man ever spoke like this man!"* That was wisdom in action.

Wisdom is self-controlled: when the jealous Jewish leaders accused him of casting out devils by the power of Satan, he did not confront them with a rage because of their blasphemy. He only warned them that they were in danger of committing the unpardonable sin. And he continued his ministry. When the unbelieving Jews sought to kill him before his time, he hid himself[85].

When Satan confronted him with his fiercest armour after his 40-day fasting, Jesus resorted to, and depended solely on, the word of God, "It is written."

When it was time for him to lay down his life for the sins of the world, he chose not to open his mouth; he became dumb like a sheep, in spite of the many malicious and atrocious false charges laid against him. God expects us also to be wise like serpents in all affairs of life and ministry, and to be gentle like doves.

Life Application

But the truth is that great men are not always wise, and even Spirit-filled men often make mistakes that put a blur not only on their integrity but also on the gospel of Christ which they preach. The excellence of wisdom prevails only when we seek to live a life of wisdom continually without turning to the left hand or to the right. May God grant us grace to be always wise and sober.

David, though a man after God's heart, and filled with the Holy Spirit, committed a terrible and foolish sin because he failed in the law of timing, and in the law of personal restraint. He stayed back in Jerusalem at a time when the army was fighting another nation. So Satan came and tempted him for his idleness. Then he killed Uriah in order to hide his shameful act. Subsequently he married his beautiful wife Bathsheba. By these unwise actions, he introduced disaster into his family.

Abraham allowed his wife, Sarah, to convince him, and he went in to Sarah's maid, Hagar, contrary to God's will for him. The birth of Ishmael is considered by some as the genesis of the rivalry over the centuries between the Arabs and the Jews.

Moses erred in uncontrolled righteous anger. He could not enter the Promised Land.

Solomon, in spite of his wisdom, went out of control in his lust for women. The same goes for Samson, and the list goes on.

King Saul went against his better judgment, and allowed the people to persuade him to disobey the clear instructions that God gave him regarding the war with Amalek; and so he lost his throne.

Demas, Paul's companion, allowed the love of this present world to becloud his judgment. He deserted Paul, and lost something of eternal value.

Friends, let us hold on to wisdom, to integrity, to truth, and let us endeavour to be sober and restrained at all times. Weigh the word you want to speak with the word of God first, before you speak it. Does it tally with the word of God? Let us use wisdom to defer anger. Let us use more discernment. Let us ask God his counsel on more of the issues of life before we embark on the projects. *"If any of you lack wisdom let him ask of God that giveth to all men liberally, and upbraideth not, and it shall be given him. But let him ask in faith, nothing doubting..."* (James 1:5).

Wisdom – The Principal Thing

Wisdom makes a man's face to shine. Wisdom does not wait to learn from experience. Rather it learns from the experiences and mistakes of others. Be wise. God is looking for wise men and women he can entrust his great work into their hands.

Some scriptural references as concerning wisdom are as follows:

> "...Look ye out among you seven men of honest report, full of the Holy Ghost and wisdom, who we may appoint over this business[86]"

> "Walk in wisdom toward them that are without[87]"

> "The price of wisdom is above rubies[88]"

> "Through wisdom is an house builded, and by understanding it is established, and by knowledge shall the chambers be filled with all precious and pleasant riches[89]"

WORK BOOK

a) Define wisdom.
b) State some ways by which we can acquire wisdom, e.g.:
   i) From God by prayer.
   ii) From the word of God by studying it.
   State 5 others.

c) Great men are not always wise. Give examples. Must you make the mistakes they made? If no, how can you avoid making the same mistakes?

d) How did Jesus overcome Satan's temptations? When you are tempted to sin, can you do likewise? How?

e) Summarize the message of this chapter in your own words.

Practical steps:

When next you are tempted to get angry, use wisdom and hold yourself. First ask God whether you should answer or forbear. If you must answer, then ask God what you should say or do. This is how wisdom starts.

THE FRUIT OF THE HOLY SPIRIT

But the fruit of the Spirit is love, joy, peace, longsuffering, gentleness, goodness, faith, meekness, temperance: against such there is no law (Galatians 5:22-23).

"...The tree is known by his fruit" (Matthew 12:33).

Thought: Aaron's rod budded, and brought forth buds, and bloomed blossoms, and yielded almonds (Numbers 17:8). It was therefore placed in the ark. Is your rod blossoming?

Christ was filled with the Spirit, walked in the Spirit, and brought forth abundant fruit of the Holy Spirit. And he says to us, *"I am the true vine, and my Father is the husbandman. Every branch in me that beareth not fruit, he taketh away; and every branch that beareth fruit he purgeth it, that it may bring forth more fruit "*(John 15:1-2).

Christ brought forth abundant fruit of:

Love

His life was love personified, and his entire ministry was pure love: love for God and love for his fellowmen, as we already discussed. He lived purely to please God in love, and loved the rest of us to the end.

Joy

In spite of the fact that he sorrowed for our sins, yet his joy was unspeakable. He rejoiced in all his tribulations for us, rejoicing in hope for our great salvation which he came to bring. He said, *"These things have I spoken unto you that my joy might remain in you, and that your joy might be full"* (John 15:11). His joy was obviously full and running over!

Peace

Christ manifested the peace of God *"which passest understanding."* Pilate was baffled by his silence and peace, at a time when his life was at stake. But why was he at peace, when everyone else was in great agitation? Because he knew his mission to the world and he trusted in his God. Christ has bequeathed to his disciples (you and I) his peace: *"Peace I leave with you. My peace I give unto you: not as the world giveth give I unto you. Let not your heart be troubled, neither let it be afraid"* (John 14:27). May you savour the peace of God today, in Jesus' name. Why? Because God is in total control of all your affairs, not the devil. Trust in God, he will bring you peace.

Longsuffering

Nowhere is the longsuffering nature of Christ more manifest than we see it at his passion. Starting with all the false accusations levelled against him, to the miscarriage of justice with all falsehood, and to the underserved punishments, beatings, maligning, and finally nailing on the cross, he opened not his mouth to defend himself, nor to bring railing accusation against the wicked perpetrators.

Can we learn from him who, though he had access to Almighty power, opened not his mouth; he allowed himself to be led as a lamb to the slaughter, for us! Let us learn the lesson of longsuffering with joyfulness in all things. Again, faith in God will enable you to suffer long without murmuring.

Gentleness

- Christ was always as gentle as a lamb.
- Right from his birth, at the stable among lambs, to his appearance at John's baptism as the Lamb of God that takes away the sins of the world, till his appearance before the throne of God in Revelation[90] to receive the Book with seven seals, the Lamb-nature never departed from the Lord Jesus Christ. Can we emulate him?

Goodness

He went about doing good, healing the sick, clothing the naked, feeding the hungry multitudes, forgiving the sinners. Christ's life radiated and reflected all goodness. So should ours.

Faith

We have pondered earlier on his faith-life. The Son of God had to walk by faith; same as the rest of us. Although God the Father indwelt him, and the Spirit descended upon him like a dove at baptism; although angels spoke to him, and God spoke audibly affirming his Sonship on the mount of transfiguration, and although he did mighty miracles by the power of the Spirit, yet the New Testament does not tell us anywhere that God appeared visibly to his Son during his time on earth as a flesh-and-blood human being. He may have, but it is not recorded. Therefore we conclude that Christ had to live by faith, and if such was required of the Son of God, then we too must follow his example.

Meekness

His meekness is seen in his restraint coupled with his strength and courage. He was even tempered. He could restrain himself when he needed to, and rule his temper in spite of his great strength.

Temperance

Christ had absolute control over his desires, appetites and passions. Can we emulate him and control our appetites and desires? Or do we give reckless vent to our appetite as soon as occasion provides for it? Remember Gideon's army? Intemperate men were disqualified.

Life Application

As the Lord said, *"Except a corn of wheat fall into the earth and die, it abideth alone: but if it dies it bringeth forth much fruit."* Except we count all things in this present world loss for Jesus and eternal life, it will be an uphill task for us to bear any meaningful fruit of the Spirit. You cannot have both heaven and this sinful world. There are many things you must let go in order to bear abundant fruit for Jesus. Fruit-bearing means a change of character, and this means that we must change our character more and more every day to resemble more closely that of Jesus, the pioneer of our faith.

To bring forth more abundant fruit of the Spirit, you will have to be a fool many times for Christ's sake. You will have to tolerate and overlook many things which you would not have tolerated in the past. And you will have to forgive many offences of people.

As you exclude from your life, and deny yourself more of those things that would have brought gain to your flesh and as you take up more and more of those things that would bring joy to the Holy Spirit, a new you will start to emerge. And as you vigorously engage in prayer, and rejoice with exceeding joy in all your tribulations, bearing the fruit of goodwill and God's love to all men, and being a good student of the word of God, your fruitfulness in the Lord will soon start to appear.

Your confidence and the joy of the Lord flowing from your life, with all the goodness of Christ will kindle a heavenly glow of beauty around your person. And men will come to enquire from you about this light of God seen in your life. What is this confident hope that you have? What is this beauty of personality that radiates from you? Why are you always filled with joy, even when things look so bleak for everybody else? What is the source of your confidence and strength? And then you will have opportunity to tell them about Jesus, the miracle-worker in your life! The joy of the Lord is your strength. Rejoice in the Lord always. And again, I say, rejoice.

WORK BOOK

a) Name as much fruit of the Spirit as you can.
b) Which ones have you excelled in, and which ones are more troublesome for you?
c) Have you ever tried to combine "longsuffering with joyfulness" as Paul admonished us? (Colossians 1:11).
d) What is meekness? And what is temperance?
e) What does it mean to be a fool for Christ's sake? (1 Corinthians 4:10).
f) Summarize the message of this chapter in your own words.

Practical steps:

How many serious offences have you forgiven others for Christ's sake within the past one week? How many have you not forgiven? Now go and forgive them.

PREACHER OF RIGHTEOUSNESS

I have preached righteousness in the great congregation: lo, I have not refrained my lips O Lord; thou knowest (Psalm 40:9).

And he said unto them, Go ye into all the world, and preach the gospel to every creature (Mark 16:15).

Thought: The world is waiting to hear from you. Speak life to the dry bones around you, and they will live.

Christ was a Preacher of righteousness in this world darkened by sin. He was an avid soul winner. He spoke to the lives of men. He spoke transformational words that men never heard before. His preaching changed the lives of men. He preached about the reality of heaven and hell, about Eternal Judgment, about sin and forgiveness of sins, about repentance, about righteousness, about death and resurrection. He spoke truths that had been kept secret from the foundation of the world. He spoke about the great love of God towards sinful mankind.

He warned sinners to repent because the Day of Judgment was coming, and the day will burn like an oven, and all the wicked will be consumed by the heat. Christ encouraged men to embrace God, truth and righteousness. He revealed that he had come from God to pay the ransom for all the sins of mankind with his own life. He urged mankind to repent and to embrace God's offer of eternal life. He announced the defeat of Satan and the hordes of hell, and the triumph of God's kingdom and the saints of God.

Great multitudes embraced the good news that he brought, and followed him. They embraced him as Lord and Saviour, and washed themselves in his blood shed at Calvary, and received his Holy Spirit sent from heaven after his resurrection. They became candidates of heaven, having been delivered from the snares of hell.

Apostolic Preaching Unabated

Today great multitudes are still following him. Why? Because his disciples, "went forth and preached everywhere, the Lord working with them, and confirming the word with signs following. Amen."[91] But wait! What if the disciples chose not to go everywhere preaching the word? What if they were satisfied just to stay in Jerusalem? Worse still, what if they felt so satisfied with their personal salvation and declined preaching to others the message of Christ? Suppose they decided just to go to fellowship and enjoy one another's company, and hear more preaching, and pray for the world to be saved by somebody else? Would we in Africa, Asia, Europe, USA, Latin America, China, India, the Pacific, Australia, and other parts of the world have heard the gospel? Would we have believed without a preacher?

The Great Commission was re-emphasized as Jesus ascended to heaven in Acts 1:8. But by Acts 8:1 the disciples were still mostly in Jerusalem. Then *"At that time there arose a great persecution against the church, which was at Jerusalem, and they were all scattered abroad throughout the regions of Judea and*

Samaria, except the apostles... then Phillip went down to the city of Samaria and preached the gospel to them."

It appears that persecution was what ignited the fire of missions, and by it they were finally able to deliver the message of Jesus to us! But must we wait for God to put burning firebrands on our tails, like Samson's three hundred foxes, before we start running with the gospel?

Life Application

All of us agree that the gospel is a wonderful, glorious, and life-saving message from heaven that should be gotten out fast to all men. It has power to open the blind eyes of men who worship stocks and trees; it will deliver the captives of Satan who are in the occult; it will cleanse and save fornicators and harlots from their sins; it will heal tottering marriages; it will bring light to those groping in darkness; it brings joy to those whose lives have been depressed by sin and Satan; it gives joy to those who are mourning, hope to the hopeless, and it will rescue those who are wallowing in the mud and gutters of life. The gospel message is transformational, life-giving, and leads multitudes of people back to God, to righteousness, and to life eternal! Praise God.

But what if we are content with just hearing the gospel, and are not interested in earnestly passing on the message to others who have not heard? What profit would it be to us, to God, and to the lost if we negligently fail to preach the gospel?

Go on Preaching: Don't Stop

The scripture declares that *"A true witness delivers souls, but a false witness speaketh lies."* The implication is that if by our words we fail to deliver the lost, then all we are speaking are lies. God called us out of the world to be his voice, a voice crying in the wilderness of this world's sin-ridden society, calling men and women to repent, and to embrace Christ and eternal life. That is the believer's primary and fundamental reason for living in this temporal world.

Eternity will soon be on us all, and God wants men saved from the fires of hell, and secured for the kingdom of God for which Christ has paid a full price. If your Christian faith has not compelled you yet to seek to save lost sinners from the fires of hell, then one would wonder if you really understand the meaning of salvation, or if you yourself are really saved.

Friends, from prophecies of scriptures, and from events happening all around us in the world today, it is evident that the end of all things is at hand. Christ is coming back soon. It is quarter to midnight in God's programme of world events. It is too late an hour for us to still say, *"The harvest is plenteous, but the labourers are few."* Where are all the people of God? Where are God's armies? Let all God's people arise, and shout a great shout of Gideon's army. And let us move into the ripe harvest and reap for God. God is depending on us (you and I).

If we do not go for God, nobody else will do it for God, *"And he that repeath receiveth wages, and gathers fruit unto life eternal, that both he that soweth and he that reapeth may rejoice together"* (John 4:36). Arise, let us get going. There is a great harvest to reap, and a great reward awaits the reapers. *"He that winneth souls is wise"* (Proverbs 11:30). *"And they that be wise shall shine as the brightness of the firmament; and they that turn many to righteousness as the stars for ever and ever"* (Daniel 12:3).

When you talk of eternal rewards, there is no work on earth that can remotely compare to soul winning: the work of bringing lost sinners back to God. That is where God made his greatest investment, by sending his only beloved Son into the world, to die for lost sinners! Let us all arise and go to reap the harvest, in Jesus' name.

WORK BOOK

a) Many people are preaching today, but how many are preaching against sin? How many are warning sinners of the dangers of hell?

b) Why must we all repent from sin? Is Judgment Day nearer than when we believed? What end-time signs can you point at?

c) If we do not preach to those around us, and they die without the gospel, will God let us go scot-free? (Ezekiel 3:17-21). Who is a watchman?

d) How do people in heathen nations hear the gospel? Must someone go to them, or do we wait for them to come to us? What does the Bible say? (Mark 16:15: Note, "Go ye").

e) When the disciples failed to go, God allowed a fiery persecution to befall the disciples. When we refuse to go what things could happen to us?

f) What rewards follow the preaching of the gospel? Name both its present and eternal benefits.

g) Summarize the message of this chapter in your own words.

Practical steps:

> "Let the dead bury their dead; but go thou and preach the kingdom of God." (Luke 9:60).

Start today, and as you win them, also disciple them.

TEMPTED, YET WITHOUT SIN

*For we have not an high priest which cannot be touched
with the feeling of our infirmities; but was in all points
tempted like as we are, yet without sin* (Hebrews 4:15).

*Blessed is the man that endureth temptation: for when
he is tried, he shall receive the crown of life which the
Lord hath promised to them that love him* (James 1:12).

Thought: Temptations, trials, and tests are for all of us; if the
devil does not tempt us, then God will surely test us, to prove
our love.

The Bible records that soon after Christ's baptism, and the
Holy Spirit alighting and resting on him, *"Immediately the
Spirit driveth him into the wilderness. And he was there in the
wilderness forty days, tempted of Satan."* It looks as if the devil
was lingering at the place of baptism, knowing that John had
prophesied about the one whose shoes' latchet he was not
worthy to stoop down to unloose. But it was not the devil that
drove him into the wilderness to be tempted.

It was the Spirit of God! It was God's idea. It seems from
the above record (and other scriptures) that God was not
sparing even his own Son from the devil's temptation. If he

was not spared from temptation then we should expect to be tempted, too! But our prayer should always be, *"Deliver us from temptation"*, as the Lord taught us to pray. It is more like, *"Deliver us from sore trial"*, because the devil's task is to tempt everybody! He also is not a respecter of persons when it comes to temptation. You would have thought he should have respected the Son of God, but he gave Jesus the greatest temptation in his armoury!

Devil Tempts, God Tests

You may ask, why does the devil tempt people, especially God's people? This question could be answered by asking another question: Why does a child who fails in an examination wish that everybody else also had failed? The answer is that he does not want to be alone in failure. He does not want to be the odd man out. So Satan does not take his failure lying low. He goes about tempting everybody else; to prove his point by getting most other people to commit sin too.

But why does God allow him? And why does God try (or test) his people? The reason God allows Satan to do his dirty work is because God really wants to screen all those who want to enter his kingdom. He wants to separate the wheat from the chaff, and since this is what Satan is doing unwittingly, God has allowed him to continue his work until the time that God has set to bring all things to conclusion.

On the other hand God tests or tries his people, not to lure them into sin, but to give them a chance to prove their love for him. The Bible shows that God does not tempt any man. However, God sets examinations for his children in order to know, and to help them also realise, how far they have gone in their walk with him.

He tested Hezekiah by withholding Isaiah the prophet from seeing Hezekiah until the ambassadors from the king of Babylon had departed. He tested Job by allowing Satan to afflict him sorely, and waiting till Satan had accomplished all his temptations before he intervened. He tested Abraham first by delaying Sarah's conception of a child, and then when the child was weaned God tested Abraham to see if he could give him back the child of promise.

In all cases of God's trials or tests, God is only seeking opportunity to show us where we are with him in obedience and fellowship, and he is looking for ways to advance us. But Satan's temptation is meant to draw us away from God and destroy us.

Life Application

In Hebrews 12:3-11, God declares that whom he loves he chastens, and that he scourges (whips) every son whom he receives. God is doing this, not to destroy us, but to perfect us in his holiness (v. 11). Therefore we must endure the tests and trials and pains that God allows us to experience in life. They are for our good, and we must go through them in faith, never allowing ourselves to be discouraged or to faint.

On the other hand Satan will try to attack every true child of God. He will try to discourage you, tempt you, and prove to God that you are not fit to inherit his kingdom. He will use people to try to discourage you, discredit you, and if possible pull down your faith. He will attack your health, business, family, marriage, and whatever. He will sow doubts in your mind about your faith, about God's love for you, and generally try to frustrate your works.

Satan will whisper to your mind that your struggle to serve God is not worth it. He will make sin appear so beautiful, and give you success stories of those who made it through ungodly short-cuts. He will try to make you sin against God, and make you to tell your children that there is no God.

Stand Your Ground

You must stand your ground. You must not pay heed to Satan's lies. You should never stay to dialogue with him. You should rebuff him repeatedly, as Christ did, with the word of God: *"It is written."* Our armouries of defence against Satan's wiles are:

1. Seek God's help.
2. Repent, and confess all known sins to God.
3. Pray earnestly with faith against Satan's attack.
4. Stand on the word of God. His word is the sharp sword of the Spirit. Keep confessing God's word for your situation no matter how bad things may look.
5. Put on the complete armour of God as shown in Ephesians 6.
6. Overcome Satan with the Blood of Christ.
7. Seek the help of other close friends in prayer. Seek also mature godly counsel.
8. Engage the infallible weapons of praise and thanksgiving, like Paul and Silas did in prison.
9. Move away from the tempting influence.
10. Resist the devil, and he will flee from you.

As you do these things, very soon the light of God will shine in your prison cell, in your situation, in whatever circumstance the devil threw you into. The Spirit of God will flood your life with God's transcendent light, and you will be set free like a bird out of the snare of the hunters. Glory! Alleluia!! Let the righteous say, *"It is well with those that serve the Lord."* In Jesus' name, Amen!

> *Blessed is the man that endureth temptation, because when he is tried, the Lord will give him the crown of life which the Lord hath promised to them that love him* (James 1:12).

WORK BOOK

a) "Temptations, trials, and tests are for all of us." Explain. What is the difference between "temptation" and "trial?"

b) Why does God permit Satan to tempt us?

c) When someone overcomes temptation, what happens to him? What is the ultimate prize for those who overcome? (Revelation 2:10, 11).

d) State ten ways that Satan tempts us?

e) What ten things must you do when you are tempted?

f) Summarize the message of this chapter in your own words.

Practical steps:

- Dissociate yourself today from the source that is currently bringing temptation to your mind.
- Remember to ask God in prayer for the grace and strength to dissociate.

THE WAY, THE TRUTH AND THE LIFE

"Jesus said to him, I am the way, the truth, and the life: no man cometh unto the Father but by me" (John 14:6).

"He that saith he abideth in him ought himself also so to walk as he walked" (1 John 2:6).

Thought: Jesus blazed a burning trail in the gospels. Follow his trail if you want to be where he is.

Jesus said he is the way, not one of the ways, to Almighty God. And he is the only way. He proved his word by living a victorious and blameless life, conquered sin and death, resurrected and ascended up to God, and is now seated at the right hand of God Almighty. He made an eternal way for those who believe in him to inherit glory and immortality.

Today there are many who claim to be the way, but they are the ways of death. Those who follow them will end up in the lake of fire, not heaven. Why? Because they do not really care for the things of God, but for their own things; and I am not talking merely of those in other world religions, or atheists, or New Agers, or pagans. I am saying that there are many people who go to church, who claim they are the real Christians, or prophets or teachers, who might even do miracles, who preach Christ but their ways leave much to be desired. They do not really care for God's truth or righteousness. They are not careful to obey God, and their lives and their message do not reflect the truth of Christ.

And all those who follow them will end up in hell, not heaven. The Lord spoke about them in Matthew 7:21-23, and also in Matthew 24:23-24. In Mark 13:6 the Lord said that *"Many shall come in my name, saying, I am Christ, and shall deceive many."* And he says we should be careful so that no one deceives us.

The Genuine Way

Friends, it is not so difficult to recognize the genuineness of the Lord. He came not to seek his own glory but God's. He did not preach about himself but was meek and lowly. He pointed men to God the Father. He went about doing good things, forgiving the sinners, and turning men to righteousness. He did not seek to build an empire for himself; instead he built men and identified with the poor and needy. He showed divine love, spoilt the works of Satan, liberated the captives of hell, and gave hope to the hopeless.

Anyone who sought to know the truth would find the truth in Christ because he came, not to take from us, but to give us everything he had, and to lay down his life for sinful men. That is why he is the Truth, the Way, and the Life. And those who follow him will be identified in the same way: by their meekness, their holy lives, and hatred for sin, by their genuine love for a lost world, their love for one another, and by their unswerving devotion to the teachings of the Lord. By their fruits you will know them.

Life Application

Friend what about you and I? Are you living the life of Christ? Can those who follow you make it to heaven? Are we walking in the steps of Christ, precept by precept? Is the divine life flowing in your life? Do you talk and walk like Jesus, do what Jesus would do? Do you live a life of truth? Or are we pretenders, running with the deer by day, and hunting with the pack at night? Are you transparent, honest, and walking in integrity? Is your yes, yes? And is your no, no? Are we double-tongued? Do we still tell lies, live in secret sins, and harbour wrong motives, harbour malice in our hearts towards others? These are the things which will prove if our testimony of Jesus is true or false, whether we are truly the servants of Jesus, or of the devil.

Today, while the Lord delays his coming, there is still opportunity for each one of us to repent. It is time to come out of the darkness, and walk in the light of God. You can become the way, the truth, and the life for someone who has lost his way to follow, and find eternal life.

God bless you for heeding.

WORK BOOK

a) Can you highlight some of the key points in the life of Christ that we need to follow in order to walk in his way?

b) How would you identify the false prophets?

c) Who is your model? Do you know any earthly models whose lives mirror that of Christ? What have you seen in them that attracts you to Christ?

d) Who are called "wolves in sheep clothing"? What are their chief interests? e.g. money, etc.

e) Are you living a transparent Christian life, or are you living a hypocritical life?

f) Summarize the message of this chapter in your own words.

Practical steps:

- Search your life, and see if there are areas of hypocrisy. Root them out of your life starting from today.

ATTRIBUTES OF CHRIST (23)

MIRACLE WORKER

"This man doeth many miracles" (John 11:47).

"Verily, verily I say unto you, he that believeth on me, the works that I do shall he do also; and greater works than these shall he do; because I go unto my Father" (John 14:12).

Thought: We have an open ticket to perform miracles, but most of us are chasing after miracles. Why?

The opposing Jewish leaders acknowledged that Christ did many miracles. Instead of glorifying God for this, it made them envious, so they plotted Christ's downfall. But the real reason for the miracles was to show God's concern for the needs of the people, and to demonstrate Christ's power over the works of Satan. These attributes showed God as the God of love and also as the Almighty God. It thus helped the people to believe that Jesus Christ was from God. Jesus said, *"Believe me that I am in the Father, and the Father in me: or else believe me for the very works' sake"* (John 14:11). The miracles helped people to believe that Jesus Christ was from God.

Life Application

Miracles in our ministries are to help people believe that the message we are preaching is of God, and the miracles serve for signs to authenticate the word. When Peter healed the palsied man at Lydda, *"All that dwelt at Lydda and Saron saw him, and turned to the Lord"* (Acts 9:35). And when Paul healed a man crippled from birth, the people at Lystra saw it, and lifted up their voices and proclaimed that *"The gods are come down to us in the likeness of men."* Miracles still continue to attract crowds to this day. And instead of criticizing the miracle workers, why do we not rather seek to work miracles ourselves?

God has promised us divers gifts of the Holy Spirit. Why are most Christians not operating in these gifts? Why are we not asking God for these gifts? How many of us are willing to forsake food and drink, even for a couple of days to seek these gifts of ministry? Granted, all may not be workers of miracles. But what about the other gifts, so many other gifts promised to us? (1Corinthians 12; Romans 12).

These gifts are necessary to enable the church to function supernaturally, as the gifts bring blessing to the church in our congregational meetings, and help us wage spiritual warfare against the forces of hell.

If we remain complacent and neglect the gifts of the Spirit we will only be functioning in the natural, and deny ourselves of the supernatural power of the Spirit. On the other hand if we seek the power, God will distribute divers gifts to us to enable the church (and us as individuals) to fulfil our ministry to the world. By casting out Satan, healing the sick, and doing other wonderful works, the early church amply demonstrated the defeat of Satan, and the power of the name of Jesus. Today's church, collectively and individually, should desire and seek that same power. It is a promise, a blessing we can no longer continue to neglect. *"Jesus Christ, the same yesterday, today, and forever"*[92]. *"Behold I and the children whom the LORD hath given me are for signs and wonders in Israel from the LORD of hosts, which dwelleth in Zion"* (Isaiah 8:18).

WORK BOOK

a) When the Lord said we would do greater miracles than he did, did he mean it? What examples, especially among the early apostles, would you consider greater miracles? (E.g. Acts 5:15, etc.).

b) Do we still see miracles today? Do you think we need many more miracles today?

c) What must we do to witness more miracles in our days?

d) Why are miracles necessary? Are you seeking for miracles?
   - Have you asked God to empower you with the gift of miracles?
   - What practical steps are you taking to receive the gift?

e) Why are many of us functioning in the natural when God has promised that he will enable us to function in the supernatural? God does not bless idle people with his spiritual gifts.

f) Summarize the message of this chapter in your own words.

Practical steps:
- Identify the service you are presently offering to the Lord through his church or fellowship.
- Ask him for divine gifts of the Spirit to help you do the work better.

ATTRIBUTES OF CHRIST (24)

HARD WORK

"They had no leisure so much as to eat." (Mark 6:31)

"In the meantime his disciples prayed him, saying, Master, eat. But he said unto them, I have meat to eat that ye know not of" (John 4:31-32).

"Know ye not that I must be about my Father's business?"

Thought: Some men will only do the Master's business if there is any left-over time from their own.

The Lord Jesus considered his Father's work top-most priority. It took all his time. There was not even enough time sometimes for him to have a decent meal. He had to preach to the multitudes who were often gathered to hear his wonderful messages and teachings; then he had to heal those who were in need of healing, pray for others, instruct and give counsel to those who were confused.

Then he had to travel to other cities, preach in their synagogues, by the sea, or on mountain tops. Then he would seek some privacy to teach the twelve, then the seventy, etc. Of course the Pharisees and chief priests and lawyers were there to ask him their hard questions. And when the crowds wanted to detain him in one city he would politely say *"No, let us go into the next towns, that I may preach there also; for therefore came I forth"* (Mark 1:38).

Christ was so engrossed with the Father's work that he would not accept excuses from would-be disciples who had their own "top" priorities. For example, when he called a man to follow him, but the man said he should be allowed "first" to go and bury his father, the Lord told him to allow the dead to bury their dead, but that he (the disciple) should go and preach the gospel.

It was as serious as that! Does it mean that Christ is against burials? No, but you know that the children of this world spend their time doing nothing more than burials, weddings, birthdays, watching movies, reading newspapers, watching TV, throwing parties, doing business, buying and selling, etc. Christ needs men who will focus on the gospel, and spread the good news to every corner of the globe!

Life Application

Christ was determined to do his Father's business and so must we. He and his twelve disciples and the one hundred and twenty in the upper room together turned their world upside down for the kingdom of God. They evangelized their entire world, including Rome. This was done in spite of persecutions, jailing, scourging, and even the killing of many of the disciples, and the opposition of mighty Rome. They laid down their lives; they went from city to city, and from nation to nation, sharing the glad tidings of the coming kingdom of God. They worked hard, and got mighty results!

What about us? How long shall we continue to be satisfied with minimal results? The results we get depend on the time and energy and speed we put into God's work: little effort, little results; big effort, big results. Why do we spend so much time on things that do not bring eternal rewards? Is it not due to lack of vision for eternal realities? Christ said to the crowd who followed him because of the miracle of bread, *"Labour not for the meat which perisheth, but for that meat which endureth unto everlasting life, which the Son of man shall give unto you: for him hath God the Father sealed"* (John 6:27).

It is lack of vision for us to spend hours daily watching television, reading newspapers, surfing the web, watching sports, socializing, or even vacationing or sleeping – and very little time is left for God and his work. Many would-be disciples of Christ do not read or study their Bibles daily, and when they do, they give it just some ten or fifteen minutes. We do not spend enough time to memorize the word, meditate and reflect on it, to see how we can apply it to our lives' situations, or how to pray with the word, or how we can discern God's will through it.

Are you fulfilling your Ministry?

Many believers have no time to pray, I mean to pray effectually and fervently to change their own lives and the lives of people around them. We often do not pray for our nations as we should. Many of us either do not know how to witness for Christ, or we are too busy to do so. We do not seem to think that sinners around us need our help to know Christ. How many believers think of missions, visitations to new converts, caring for the elderly and down-trodden, teaching in Sunday school in church, prison or hospital visitations, or starting a home-fellowship for people in our neighbourhood?

How many of us are regular in going to pray for the sick, or practising the true religion, which according to apostle James, is *"To visit the fatherless and widows in their affliction, and to keep oneself unspotted from the world?"*[93]

Friends, let us arise together and do the works of him that sent us. The Great Commission is for us to go to the ends of the earth with the glad tidings of Christ; but if we cannot go to the ends of the world, let us at least make some impact for God in our neighbourhoods, our villages, offices, churches, families, and our cities. Let us carve out some prime times daily, or weekly, when we can put our hands to the plough, and do some commendable work for God's kingdom.

For what will it profit a man if he shall gain the whole world, and have little or no rewards in God's coming eternal kingdom? *"For the kingdom of heaven is like unto a man that is an householder, which went out early in the morning to hire labourers into his vineyard. And when he had agreed with the labourers for a penny a day, he sent them into his vineyard... So when even was come, the Lord of the vineyard saith unto his steward, Call the labourers, and give them their hire, beginning from the last unto the first"* (Matthew 20:1, 2, 8).

The point here is that we are saved to serve in God's vast vineyard and the Lord promises to pay us based on how we serve. Little service, little eternal remuneration; much service: much eternal remuneration. Jesus worked hard to complete his divinely-approved assignment. So should we, but it seems likely that many saints may have hidden their talents. Let us work hard for God. His work is the only work that carries eternal rewards with it.

WORK BOOK

a) Why did Christ work so hard? What about us? What are the usual things that occupy the times of most people?

b) Do you devote any time to go and do God's work, or are you a mere fellowship Christian?

c) Which area of ministry do you occupy for the Lord? How effective are you?

d) How many souls have you brought to Christ within the past six months? Are they being trained to be Disciples of Christ?

e) God will pay those who work for him, for he says, *"The Labourer is worthy of his hire."* How do you think your payment will be like in eternity?

f) Summarize the message of this chapter in your own words.

Practical steps:

Prayerfully identify an area of ministry that is lacking in the church. Then go and fulfil it.

ATTRIBUTES OF CHRIST (25)

PRAISE

"And when they had sung a hymn (psalm), they went out into the mount of Olives" (Mark 14:26).

"And at midnight Paul and Silas prayed, and sang praises unto God: and the prisoners heard them" (Acts 16:25).

"Who is like unto thee, O LORD, among the gods? Who is like thee, glorious in holiness, fearful in praises, doing wonders?" (Exodus 15:11).

Thought: Genuine praise elates us, and makes us feel like doing more. I wonder if God feels like that too.

Christ, after the Passover supper, on the same night when he was arrested, sang praises to God with his disciples. Is it not amazing that in spite of what he knew he would go through, he still could afford to sing praise to God that night? Jesus knew the power of praise and thanksgiving. He knew the power of praise to unlock heaven, and release the awesome power of God. God is fearful in praises, so Christ praised him on that dark night.

He declared God's glory, power and majesty over all the earth, over hell, over principalities and powers, and over creation. He did not allow his circumstances to weigh down his spirit. He praised God for his wisdom, power, and love and for being in total control over all things. By his praise he disarmed the forces of hell, and gave due glory to God Almighty for everything that was to take place in the coming hours and days. And heaven took notice.

Life Application

If ever there was a time to give God praise, the best time that heaven would appreciate it is at those times when all hell seems to be let loose, when we seem helpless, when hell thinks it has triumphed.

That is the best time to deflate Satan's ego, and cause heaven to applaud us. Praise sends signals to God that we know he is in control, he has not forgotten us, he is working out his purpose in our lives, and we will love him to the end, no matter what happens!

In Acts 16:23 Paul and Silas had suffered humiliation of imprisonment and beatings. Their backs were torn with stripes and their feet locked in stocks, yet in the midst of all these, they sang out praises unto God Almighty for his goodness and mercy. The prisoners heard them singing, but no one could understand why and how they could sing under such circumstances – until God invaded their prison! *"There was a great earthquake, so that the foundations of the prison were shaken: and immediately all the doors were opened, and everyone's bands were loosed"* (v. 26). God is indeed fearful, awesome, in praises!

Friends, let us praise God more. There is no circumstance of our lives that he is not aware of. He is working out everything for good for those who love God and keep his commandments. Even in your darkest midnight dare to sing praise to God. Dare to extol his goodness, power, wisdom, and love. God will arise for you.

When King Jehoshaphat and the people of Israel were surrounded by their enemies and all hope seemed lost, they sought God by fasting and prayers. God responded by instructing them to go before the invading army with songs of praise unto him, *"For he is good, and his mercies endureth for ever."* And as they obeyed God in faith, God arose and destroyed all the armies that had surrounded their city. He will save and deliver you, too. And if he does not do it for your praises, certainly murmuring and complaining and depression will not move him, for the joy of the Lord is your strength.

Exhortation to Praise

The Psalms form the longest single book in the Bible. Many of them were sung in the days of David's troubles. He sang and praised God even when his life was endangered by King Saul and other enemies. Is it a wonder, then, that in each case God marvellously delivered him? And he was called a man after God's heart? He knew how to arouse God to action!

God has a grand plan for your life. He made you for his own purpose, and for his own glory. Let us therefore commit our lives unto him for safe-keeping, as unto a faithful Creator.

> Let the saints be joyful in glory: let them sing aloud upon their beds. Let the high praises of God be in their mouth, and a two-edged sword in their hand; to execute vengeance upon the heathen, and punishments upon the people; to bind their kings with chains, and their nobles with fetters of iron; to execute the judgment that is written: this honour have all his saints. Praise ye the LORD (Psalm 149:5-9).

- What time I am afraid, I will trust in thee, in God I will praise his word (Psalm 56:3)
- Praise is comely for the upright (Psalm 33:1)
- I will bless the Lord at all times; his praise shall continually be in my mouth (Psalm 34:1)
- Whosoever offers praise glorifies me... (Psalm 50:23)
- Enter into his gates with thanksgiving, and into his courts with praise; be thankful unto him and bless his name (Psalm 100:4)
- Have ye never read, out of the mouth of babes and suckling thou has perfected praise? (Matthew 21:16)
- Praise ye the LORD. Praise the LORD, O my soul. While I live, I will praise the LORD: I will sing praises unto my God while I have any being (Psalm 146:1-2)
- Oh that men would praise the Lord for his goodness... (Psalm 107:8).

WORK BOOK

a) It is easy to sing praises when God has done you some special favours. But it takes faith to sing and praise him in your dark night with troubles all around. That is when praise becomes a demonstration of faith. That is when heaven takes more notice. Have you ever tried it? Abraham did it at 99 years of age, and without a child from Sarah, giving glory to God (Romans 4:20).

b) How do you feel when genuine praise is given you, especially when you do not think you have done so well? Does it not make you feel encouraged to do even more? What about God?

c) List some reasons why all men should praise God continually. List reasons why you especially should praise him.

d) God is fearful in praises (Exodus 15:11). Give biblical examples. Do you have personal examples?

e) When David sang praises and played with his instrument, the evil spirit departed from King Saul. Why do you think this happened? Don't evil spirits like music that praises God? How can you apply this to your own life?

f) Summarize the message of this chapter in your own words.

Practical steps:

When next you feel helpless, boxed in, confused… try singing praises, and exalting God's name, wisdom, power, etc., in spite of how you feel anyway, and see what God will do. Just give him time, and continue to praise and thank him for his wonderful deliverance and mercies, until it comes. It will surely come at the end and in time too.

CRUCIFIED TO THE WORLD

I lay down my life for the sheep... No man taketh it from me, but I lay it down of myself. I have power to lay it down, and I have power to take it up again. This commandment have I received of my Father (John 10:15-18).

I am crucified with Christ: nevertheless I live; yet not I, but Christ liveth in me: and the life which I now live in the flesh I live by the faith of the Son of God who loved me, and gave himself for me (Galatians 2:20).

Thought: The flesh and the Spirit are in mortal combat, and you are the umpire. The winner is determined by you.

Christ was crucified about two thousand years ago at Calvary, near Jerusalem. But in God's dispensation and foreknowledge, he was *"The Lamb slain from the foundation of the world."* (Revelation 13:8). His death was a decision mutually agreed upon by all members of the Godhead from the beginning. Christ clearly revealed that he was not forced to die for mankind's sins. He died by his own consent. It was love that compelled him; love to do his Father's will, and love to save us.

Therefore he willingly played into the hands of the Jews, their High Priests, Herod, Pilate, and others. Why? Because he wanted to deliver us from eternal consequences of sin: death in hellfire; he wanted to give us eternal life and joy in God's eternal kingdom. He wanted to beget more children for God. Although crucifixion was a tortuous and dreadful ordeal, he had accepted it of his own free-will before the actual crucifixion. Otherwise he had powers, up till the last minute, to refuse, and to call upon God to send him warring angels from heaven to deliver him.

Then Christ said that we also should follow his steps. In fact he gives our self-crucifixion as a pre-condition that must be met before we can truly be accepted as one of his disciples. *"And he that taketh not his cross, and followeth after me, is not worthy of me"* (Matthew 10:38). What are the implications of this for every disciple of Christ?

Life Application

1. We should be instructed not to love this present life too much. Even though this life is precious and should be treasured, yet we must always remember that it is temporal, it is imperfect, it will cease someday. It is not immortal but material and corruptible... There is a better life, a higher life, an immortal life which Christ has promised to those who love him. And he is coming back for us with that incorruptible and glorious heavenly body on the day of rapture, or resurrection. So we should be willing to give up this earthly tabernacle if God desires it to be so.

2. We should not hold too tightly to any of the things of this world: whether money, houses, children, spouse, friends, or any other thing, *"For we brought nothing into this world, and it is certain we can carry nothing out"* (1Timothy 6:7). We are pilgrims here.

3. Most importantly we are called upon to crucify our old man, the flesh, the first Adam's nature within us, for *"Our old man is crucified with Christ." "Mortify therefore your members which are upon the earth: fornication, uncleanness, inordinate affection, evil desires, and covetousness, which is idolatry"* (Colossians 3:5). Let us nail them up on the cross of Christ, through the help of the Holy Spirit. *"But God forbid that I should glory, save in the cross of our Lord Jesus Christ, by whom the world is crucified unto me, and I unto the world"* (Galatians 6:14). Is your old nature crucified?

Go for Complete Crucifixion

Paul said, *"I am crucified with Christ: nevertheless I live; yet not I, but Christ liveth in me..."* It is a statement we can all recite easily and often and yet remain un-crucified. But for Paul, he meant every word of it: not only was he crucified because Christ was crucified on his behalf, but in actual fact, by his present life-style and personal resolution Paul now reckoned himself dead indeed to self and to the things of this world. He was resolved to live only for God, for the gospel, and no longer for himself, or for men, or any personal goals. He saw himself as a purchased possession for God's use only. He had given himself away as an offering to the Lord who died and rose again from the dead for him. From henceforth he (Paul) would live only for him.

Friends, we need to come to that same resolution and revelation concerning our lives. Our lives are not really ours anymore. Our old life was doomed for destruction in hell because of sin. But Jesus came and paid the price for our sins, and gave us a new lease of life to be lived in him! He took us to the cross, we were crucified with him, and then in his resurrection he raised us up with himself, took us to heavenly places in himself, and made us to sit with him, and blessed us there with heavenly blessings. And now he has sent us to earth as men to accomplish a work for him. We can no longer live unto ourselves because our lives are not ours but his.

> *Even when we were dead in sins, he hath quickened us together with Christ, (by grace ye are saved), and hath raised us up together, and made us sit together in heavenly places in Christ Jesus.*

Thus the call for us to crucify ourselves, and mortify our members which are upon the earth, is a serious call with full justification, for Christ our Passover has been sacrificed for us, and our new lives are hid in Christ. Our lives now will find meaning only as we live wholly for him.

WORK BOOK

a) *"The Spirit and the flesh are in mortal combat, and you are the umpire"* (Galatians 5:16-18). Explain this statement.

b) Are you truly crucified? In which areas of your life is your flesh still active?

c) Christ had made up his mind to die for the world before he came into the world. But as the time approached there was crisis at Gethsemane. Why?

d) How can we defeat the flesh, and do the will of God? How did Christ do it?

e) A dead man has let go everything he possessed. What are you still holding on to that could have been used to further the cause of Christ?

f) Summarize the message of this chapter in your own words.

Practical steps:

It will take God to convince us that our lives are no longer really ours, but God's. Therefore start praying from today that God will give you a personal revelation of what it means to be *"crucified with Christ."*

RESURRECTION LIFE

"I am He who lives, and was dead, and behold, I am alive forevermore. Amen. And I have the keys of Hades and of Death" (Revelation 1:18, NKJV).

"...Ye are risen with him through the faith of the operation of God..." (Colossians 2:12)

"Ye are of God, little children, and have overcome them: because greater is he who is in you than he who is in the world" (1 John 4:4).

Thought: Our greatest prayer should be that Christ will live in us; that he be manifested through our mortal bodies to our world.

Many more Christians need to know and appreciate that Christ is not dead but he is alive and well. He is alive forevermore! He is no longer in the grave but he is risen and ascended to the heavens. Yea, and not only so, but he has sent his Spirit upon men on earth – upon us who believe in him. His Spirit is his power, his dominion, his glory, his divine abilities, his presence and his grace. And his Spirit imparts divine gifts to his own. Indeed, *"the Lord is that Spirit"* (2 Corinthians 3:17).

We are not at the mercy of the devil and the world. We are no longer under the dominion of sin.

The risen Christ has chosen to make us his dwelling place. We are God's abode, his address, his people, his sons and daughters. He is working in us, and through us he will subdue the world, principalities and powers, and all the hosts of Satan. Through the church he wants to teach principalities the manifest counsels of God[94].

The greatest lesson that we can learn today is that the risen Christ is not only sitting at the right hand of God Almighty, interceding for us, but that he also indwells us. He is with us, he has not deserted us. He is doing something wonderful within us, and through us. And when he finishes with us we shall be made purer and more precious than gold! He says to each one of us, *"All power is given unto me in heaven and in earth. Go ye therefore, and teach all nations... And lo I am with you always, even unto the end of the world. Amen"* (Matthew 28:18-20). What are the implications of all these?

Life Application

1. We need to develop a greater awareness of he who indwells us. We should passionately court his presence, his friendship, and get to know him more and more, and seek to be like him who first loved us.

2. We need to commune more with him, and have more fellowship with him. He is a living Person, and he loves us and desires to speak with us and through us to our world. Let us not try to put him in one part of his house. He is God. He should take full control of his temple.

3. We should abolish all fear, especially the fear of death. Why? Because Jesus has *"the keys of hell and of death"*[95],

not the devil; so no man can kill us, no, no devil can, until it pleases Christ to call us home. Alleluia. The Psalmist said, *"I shall not die but live, and declare the works of the Lord"* (Psalm 118:17).

4. Since he is doing a glorious work of transformation within us, let us yield to him. Let him, through his indwelling Spirit, thoroughly put to death the fleshly old sinful nature within us, and present us as a pure and holy lump before God.

5. Let us seek to manifest more and more of his divine nature and his righteousness to our world. Then men will start to call upon the name of the Lord because of us.

6. Let us walk more and more in his divine power, and through his enabling grace subdue and dominate our environment for him: all spheres of life, whether the economy, the media, the government, the educational sector, and every other sector where it pleases him to place us. We can do so because the scriptures declare that we are more than conquerors through him.

7. And let us go forth into all nations with his precious life-giving gospel as he instructed us. No man can stop us if he be with us, for with God all things are possible. And as we go for him, clothed with the garment of his righteousness and the Spirit of truth and soberness, we will trust him to authenticate the word we speak with signs and wonders following.

Glory to God! He is alive and with us, and we are like arrows in the hands of this mighty Man. Alleluia.

> *Behold, I give unto you power to tread on serpents and*
> *scorpions, and over all the power of the enemy: and*
> *nothing shall by any means hurt you* (Luke 10:19).

WORK BOOK

a) What does it mean to live the resurrection life? Can you explain this statement, *"Christ in you, your hope of glory"* (Colossians 1:27).

b) If Christ indwells us, why do many Christians still fear the occult, fear devils, fear men, and fear many other "fears"?

c) Does "Christ in us" absolve us from temptations, difficulties, troubles, etc., that are "common to man?" (1 Corinthians 10:13). What should we do in such cases?

d) *"For whatsoever is born of God overcometh the world and this is the victory that overcometh the world, even our faith"* (1 John 5:4). Explain.

e) How can we develop a greater awareness of him who indwells us? (See previous teaching on His Presence).

f) Summarize the message of this chapter in your own words.

Practical steps:

The key to this glorious level of life is to carry a constant consciousness of his divine Presence. Continue to pray for it, and practise it.

SPIRIT OF THANKSGIVING

"... Father, I thank thee that thou hast heard me..."
(John 11:41). {*Lazarus was still dead in the grave when*
Jesus gave thanks to God.}

"And Jesus took the loaves, and after he had given
thanks, he distributed to the disciples and the disciples
to them that were set down..." (John 6:11).

"And he took the cup, and when he had given thanks,
he gave it to them..." (Mk 14:23).

Thought: Christ's custom was to give God thanks for everything. He even gave Him thanks for the cup of wine that symbolized his imminent sufferings and agony at Calvary.

It is said that God loves a cheerful giver. But without doubt God also loves a grateful receiver. Many people receive from him, but how many show appreciation to him for all his wonderful goodness to the sons of men? He makes his sun to shine on the just and the unjust, and his rain to fall for all men also. But how often is God appreciated for all his goodness? Many times we complain about these great endowments of his love if we feel that our personal programs are in any way upset by these his blessings!

Christ had a wonderful spirit of gratitude to his Father-God. In all things he saw the good hand of God on his life, whether those things seemed palatable or not. He thanked God always for all things that befell him, and yielded to God's will. Before his passion, he thanked God at the breaking of bread and the pouring of wine, symbolizing his suffering. He rejoiced and thanked God the Father that his disciples' names (and ours) are written in heaven (Luke 10:21). Before he raised Lazarus from the dead, he thanked God. Before he broke bread to feed thousands of followers, he thanked God. On the Emmaus road, after his resurrection, his disciples recognized him at the breaking of bread by his usual way of blessing and thanking God.

Heavenly Host Thank God

The Book of Revelation shows that all the hosts of heaven give thanks continuously to God for all his greatness, power, wisdom, might, majesty and dominion.

Rev. 4:9: This scripture shows that the four living creatures round about God's throne give God thanks continually before the throne.

Rev. 11:16, 17: The twenty-four elders before the throne fell on their faces and worshipped God saying, We give thee thanks, O Lord God Almighty, which art, and was and is to come...

Rev. 7:11, 12: And all the angels stood round about the throne... and worshipped saying... thanksgiving...

Rev. 7:9, 10: A great multitude which no man could number of all nations and kindred and peoples, and tongues stood before the throne... and cried, saying, Salvation to our God which sitteth on the throne, and unto the Lamb.

Saints of Old Gave Thanks

Daniel prayed and gave God thanks three times a day (Dan 6:10).

David's Psalms were mostly songs of thanksgiving and appreciation to God for his wonderful goodness to the sons of men. The Psalms are the single longest book in the Bible. We are admonished to enter his gates with thanksgiving (Ps 95:2, 100:4), and his courts with praises.

Abraham, Isaac and Jacob built altars as memorials of thanksgiving for God's goodness and protection.

All the prophets of old appreciated God for his wonderful works to the children of men. David admonished that even the trees should clap their hands to God, and the mountains jump like rams in appreciation of God's awesome greatness.

Peter taught us that it is thankworthy if a man for conscience toward God endure grief, suffering wrongfully (1 Pet 2:19).

After the apostles had been beaten by the Sanhedrin, they came to their own company and rejoiced and thanked God that they were accounted worthy to suffer for the name of Christ. God responded by causing an earthquake that shook the building they were in, and giving them another endowment of Holy Ghost power and anointing (Acts 4:41).

Paul admonishes that: "In everything give thanks; for this is the will of God in Christ Jesus concerning you" (1 Thessalonians 5:18). And when they were seriously beaten with many stripes and thrown into prison in Philippi, both he and Silas prayed and sang praises and thanked God in prison. God responded by performing a miracle and setting them free from their chains.

Life Application

Let us, like Christ and his apostles, like all the hosts of heaven, and like the prophets of old, also learn **in everything** to give God thanks. He knows us, and we cannot be hidden from His presence. If we take the wings of the morning and fly to the uttermost parts of the islands, God is there. If we ascend to heaven, or descend into hades, he is there waiting for us. He says we are the apple of His eyes and that he will never leave us nor forsake us.

Such love is too wonderful for us to comprehend.

He cares for us and supplies our daily needs.

He protects us round about, and like a mother-eagle he dotes over us, and bears us on his wings.

He has put us in his secret place, and under his everlasting arms shall we trust. He has hidden us in his Son Jesus Christ, even the Son of his bosom. Thus we can boldly say: The Lord is our helper, and we shall not fear; what can men do to us? Friends, above all things, we must thank God always that our names are written in the Lamb's book of life. Jesus said to his disciples: Rejoice not that the devils are subject to you, but rejoice rather that your names are written in heaven (Luke 10:20).

Friends, let us appreciate God's goodness continually in spite of the travails or troubles that often assail us. Scriptures declare that even those worrisome troubles are for our good, because **all things** work together for good to those who are the called according to God's purpose (Rom 8:28).

> For our light affliction which is but for a moment,
> worketh for us a far more exceeding and eternal
> weight of glory (2 Corinthians 4:17).

By him therefore let us offer the sacrifice of praise
to God continually, that is, the fruit of our lips,
giving thanks to his name (Hebrews 13:15)

Jesus healed ten lepers, and expected them to return to give God thanks, but, alas, only one returned (Luke 17:17). May God grant us grace, that each one of us will be that grateful servant who keeps returning daily, to give glory and thanks to God for his unspeakable gift, for his care over our lives; and the unseen battles he fights for us every day.

God loves a cheerful giver... of gratitude in all things. He is mighty when we give him thanks!

Give him thanks with godly living.

Give him thanks with praises.

Give him gifts, money, houses, cars and applauses.

Give testimonies of his goodness.

Give him thanks in times of trials and scarcity.

Give him thanks in times of peace and plenty.

Give him thanks in anticipation of his great deliverance.

Give him thanks for what he has done.

Thank him for the wonderful things he will yet do.

When you do not understand what's going on anymore, just thank him.

By all means, and in everything, give God thanks!

THANK YOU, LORD GOD ALMIGHTY, WHO WAS, WHO IS, AND WHO IS TO COME! We love and appreciate you, Jesus, thou Son of the Living God! Thank you for being there for us at all times, and in every situation. Thank you, Lord!

WORK BOOK

a) Does God deserve thanksgiving from us? Give at least 10 reasons why?

b) What about during the "bad times"? Why must we give thanks to him when things are no longer at ease?

c) Disaster after disaster struck Job. Yet he said "Blessed be the name of the Lord" (Job 1:21). What can we learn from Job's experiences?

d) Before the creative miracles of raising Lazarus from the dead, and feeding of 5,000 men with five loaves of bread, Jesus thanked the Lord. How can we explain this thanksgiving? Can we emulate him?

e) Can we learn anything from the heavenly host who praise and give God thanks continually, without ceasing?

f) In what ways can you give God thanks?

g) What is the greatest thing that God has done for you?

h) Summarize the message of this chapter in your own words.

Practical steps:

Practise praising and thanking God as the heavenly hosts do – continually, every day, in everything, without ceasing. It will change your life forever!

CHAPTER FIVE

THE COST OF DISCIPLESHIP

And there went great multitudes with him, and he turned and said unto them, If any man come to me and hate not his father and mother, and wife and children, and brethren, and sisters, yea, and his own life also, he cannot be my disciple. For which of you, intending to build a tower, sitteth not down first, and counteth the cost, whether he has sufficient to finish it? (Luke 14:25-28).

Thought: Before any of us thinks the cost of following Christ is unbearable, it is wise also to count the cost of not following him.

It is wonderful to know that God's will is for us to be conformed to the image of Christ. We have also seen the need for us to undergo discipleship in order to be conformed to his image. Studying his divine attributes has been enriching, enlightening, and very rewarding. But one thing remains to be done, and without doing it, all we have done so far will be as if nothing has been done yet: WE NEED TO TAKE ACTION. We need to pay the price of discipleship, by actually adopting what we have learnt, practising them, and making them our own. We need to practise and imbibe Christ's attributes, and make them ours. There are seven things we must do to actualise God's dream of Christian discipleship for our lives.

1. **Repentance**

   We must acknowledge that we have fallen short of God's prescribed standard for us. No matter how good we may have been compared to those around us, we must ask the Holy Spirit to convict us of more of our familiar sins, or besetting sins, or presumptuous sins. It was the Holy Spirit that convicted prophet Isaiah of the need to cleanse his unclean lips.

   Nobody could have done that for him because he was already a great prophet carrying God's message of "Woe" to the sinful nation. Likewise, if we ask God, he will convince us of areas of our lives where we need to repent, and he will also sanctify us.

   In the book of Revelation God sent his messages to the seven churches in Asia. In each case, he was commending and rebuking his people.

   In one of the cases, he even threatened to take away the candlestick of a particular church from its place. For others, he threatened to blot their names from the book of life, if they did not repent (Revelation 3:5). These were all God's people whom he loved, just like us. Therefore if we desire to become the ultimate disciples that God wants us to be, we should put away our pride, and ask God to show us our sins. We should also be ready to repent if he shows us.

2. **Create Time / Be Determined**

   You must be determined and committed in your quest to grow in Christ's image and stature. Earnestly seek divine assistance in this matter because it is not by power, nor by might, but by the Spirit of the Lord. We should seek this divine attainment as for hidden treasure, for the Lord says that those who seek him earnestly will find him. *"...Be diligent that ye may be found of him without spot, and blameless"* (2 Peter 3:14). You will need to devote time to seek this great virtue (Christlikeness). You cannot accomplish the feat if you devote most of your time to watching secular TV, soccer, movies, or in the pursuit of money and business. Athletes devote time to practice, and world champions are those who have given their lives to much practice. Practice makes perfect, even in the matter of godliness also.

3. **Prayers**

   Since growth in Christlikeness will be attained only through the help of God, it means that we have to seek God earnestly in prayers. It has been noted that prayerless Christians are powerless Christians; similarly, those who are spiritual are those who engage God more in prayers. It was after Moses had been in the presence of God for forty days that his face shone. May your face shine with the light of God, in Jesus' name, Amen!

4. **Study of God's Word**

   To grow into Christ's likeness we must see him as he is. Through the study of the scriptures, especially the gospels and the epistles, we will discern more of his nature, character, ministry, likes and dislikes, and his teachings. There are men of God who have memorized the entire gospels of Christ. And others, like Finis Dakes, have memorized the entire New Testament. The more you study and meditate on the life of Christ, the more insight you will gain into his life and ministry, and the more you will resemble him.

5. **Carry Your Cross**

Christ says that if we want to be his disciples, we must carry our crosses, and follow him. The cross is an instrument of crucifixion. This means that if you want to become like Jesus in this world of sin, you must be prepared to suffer for it, and be ready, if necessary, to die also. The scriptures declare plainly that Satan is "the god of this world", and also the prince that now governs the lives of the children of darkness. This present evil world is described as the enemy of God, and, in alignment with the devil, the world's people caused the death of Christ and his apostles, and martyred the saints of God down through many generations from the days of Abel and Cain to the present time.

There is no way you can befriend God and the world at the same time because they are perpetual enemies. Even though God so loved the world that he gave his only Son to die for the sins of the world, yet *"friendship with the world is enmity against God."* We are pilgrims passing through this world. We will endeavour to win the world back to God, but should never partake in their sinful ways. And because of your refusal to partake in the world's ways, it will surely persecute you.

But the scriptures declare that, *"If we suffer with Christ, we shall reign with him"*, and, *"He that endureth to the end shall be saved."*[96] In fact, carrying your cross means suffering, and sometimes suffering unto death[97].

6. **Hate your Father and Mother and Wife and Children…**
   All that the Lord is saying here is that you (an aspiring disciple of Christ who wants to grow into his image and stature) must love your closest relations far less than you love Christ and God. This is understandable because your unbelieving relatives, parents, spouses, children and friends are the ones who wield the most power to influence your decisions and goals in life. God does not want to compete with them, because he made you and them. And he wants you to serve and worship him alone, for he is your God, and has great things in store for you that no parents or spouse or children or friends can ever give you. Moreover he has done for you what no man can ever do for you: he gave his only Son, Jesus Christ, to die for you, to cleanse you from your sins, and to give you eternal life.

7. **Obedience**
   "Then said Jesus to those Jews which believed on him: If ye continue in my word, then are ye my disciples indeed" (John 8:31). The ultimate test of true discipleship is obeying the Lord. As we embark on the spiritual discipline of following and emulating the Lord, what will help us to make spiritual progress is obedience. We must obey what the Spirit teaches us. And we must obey what the word says. Then the Lord will be pleased to transform us into his image and stature. No amount of sacrifice or service we render to God will ever take the place of obedience to God's word, for, *"Obedience is better than sacrifice"*[98].

From the scripture quoted earlier (John 8:31) it is evident that mere believing in Christ is not enough. Many of those Jews who believed in Jesus later turned around to stone the same Jesus whom they purportedly believed in (see John 8:40 & 59). And today it is still not different from what was then: many believers still deny Jesus and crucify him afresh by living lives of disobedience. *"They profess that they know God, but in works they deny him, being abominable and disobedient, and unto every good work reprobate"* (Titus 1:16).

Obedience remains a key test of our discipleship and love for God. *"Why call me Lord, Lord, and keep not my commandment?"*

> *He that hath my commandments and keepeth them, he it is that loveth me; and he that loveth me shall be loved of my Father, and I will love him, and will manifest myself to him* (John 14:21).

WORK BOOK

a) Has God shown you any areas you need to show true repentance? If not, ask him.
b) Will you carve out time from your busy worldly schedules to grow in grace? What will you expunge from your daily routine?
c) Determine now how you intend to study the word of God this year.
d) Are there people you love more than Jesus in this world, for example, your boyfriend or girlfriend? That is idolatry.

e) When obedience involves suffering, do you find an easy way out? That is compromise.

f) Summarize the message of this chapter in your own words.

Practical steps:

Resolve today to pay the full price required to be a true disciple of Christ.

DIFFICULT AREAS

A disciple's training is not complete without tests, trials and temptations. Even Christ was tempted, and none of us is exempt from temptations. We are expected to overcome in every area of life, because Christ has made us more than conquerors, and he lives within us to help us. He ever lives with the Father to make intercessions for us in all our trials.

Nevertheless there are areas of life where many of us often tend to miss the mark in our relationship with God, and we want to highlight some of the more common areas, and proffer possible remedies for victory for every disciple.

The Bible declares very clearly that only "overcomers" will inherit the kingdom of God (Revelation 2:7, 11). What are we expected to overcome?

CHAPTER SIX

MONEY MATTERS AND MAMMON

"...Money answereth all things" (Ecclessiastes 10:19)

"Ye cannot serve God and mammon" (Matthew 6:24)

"For the love of money is the root of all evil..." (1Timothy 6:10)

Thought: Money will demand the love and service (devotion) which should be reserved for God alone.

The Scriptures acknowledge the power of money to answer all things. There is no known area of life where money does not change hands in transactions. You need it for food, water, shelter, transport, childbirth, child-rearing, marriage, business, leisure, gifts, and name it... The usefulness of money cannot be overemphasized. Even in offering God true worship we need money. Virtually every sacrifice we offer has a monetary value.

Money speaks. With it you can solve many problems in life. Without it problems compound, without money people will look down on you, but with money even the mean man is given undue esteem by many.

Now, because of the value of money in daily human affairs, money (especially its acquisition) has been abused by many in our world. Some people will do almost anything to acquire money. Apart from stealing, robbery and prostitution there are many other despicable things that many people do in the quest of acquisition of money. Recently we saw on television how (in a certain Asian country) some gangs of boys inflict grievous harm on young children and cripple them, and then turn them into street beggars so that they can make money out of them.

The devil, knowing the value of money, has used it as a very successful tool for holding many people in sin's bondage. It is one of his most formidable tools in turning many people (even would-be disciples) away from the kingdom of God.

Bible Warnings on Money

God is not silent on the power and the abuse of money. He has warned us that we cannot serve him and mammon. This implies that some people deify money, and would do anything for money. Some will sell their souls to make money, but God says that every true believer should be careful of how he makes his money. Do not make unscrupulous money and hope to use it to serve God. God will not accept it. God will reject both the money and the person who brings it as unclean.

He says, *"I hate robbery for burnt offering"* (Isaiah 61:8). Again God says we are not to bring the wares of a harlot or the price of a dog (an unclean animal) into his house for offering[99]. These are very clear instructions. Be careful of how you make your money. Do not use unclean money (made from bribery and corruption, and such like), to serve God, because he will not accept it. God calls money generally as the mammon of unrighteousness (Luke 16:11) because of the general tendency to make money through ungodly means.

Christ warned his followers against covetousness, emphasizing that a man's life does not consist in the abundance of the things which he possesses[100]. It was because of money that Judas betrayed the Lord Jesus. Peter rebuked a "converted" Simon the sorcerer who tried to purchase the gift of God with money, *"Thy money perish with thee"* [101].

Paul warns us about the love of money:

> *And they that will be rich fall into temptation and a snare and into many foolish and hurtful lusts, which drown men in destruction and perdition. For the love of money is the root of all evil: which while some coveted after, they have erred from the faith, and pierced themselves through with many sorrows* (1Timothy 6:9-10).

Remember also that Abraham, after defeating the kings of Canaan in battle, declined to receive the gifts from the king of Sodom. Why? *"...lest thou should say, I have made Abram rich"* (Read Genesis 14:21-24).

A true man of God, a true disciple of Christ, must take heed to these words. Take heed how you make your money. Money may answer all things, but money is not everything. Do not allow unclean money to spoil your relationship with God.

Finally remember also Ananias and Sapphira. They were a prominent example to the early church on how not to be covetous or crafty. They sold their own land and brought part of the money to the church to meet the needs of the church. But they made false declarations on how much they actually sold the land.

They desired praise, but coveted part of the money, and died for it. It was a double burial for double covetousness.

God is warning his church against covetousness, and every would-be disciple should take note. What interests God most is not necessarily the size of the money we give him but the heart of the giver. The Lord Jesus commended the widow who gave a farthing, and said that she gave more than everybody else. Why? Because she gave all her livelihood even though it was just a farthing; may God help us to be disciples, indeed!

Advice on Money

- Do not love gifts (bribes) because they blind the eyes of the wise[102]. Do not give and do not take.
- Be circumspect. It is not every gift (whether money or not) that you must accept.
- It is not every gift (whether money or not) that God accepts.
- Be careful about your source of making money. Be sure it is divinely approved.
- Do not engage in fraudulent practices to make money.
- Do not tell lies because of money.
- Do not love money or covet it.
- Do not defile yourself or your business with accursed money, like Achan.
- Do not eat your tithes.
- Covetousness kills at the end.
- Be accountable; render correct account in every business or transaction as unto the Lord. If you serve God sincerely with the little you have genuinely earned, he will increase it with time. God is faithful.

WORK BOOK

a) Does money require service? Do people love money?
   Do you?
b) How do people worship money, and why?
c) Compare the time you devote for making money to the
   time you spend in serving God. Critically evaluate how
   many hours you spend each week for money / business
   matters, and compare it to the hours you spend each
   week for God's things.
d) What warnings does God give us about money? What
   is unrighteous mammon? (Luke 16:11).
e) Discuss unscrupulous ways by which even believers
   make money these days. Will God accepts such gifts?
   (Isaiah 61:8).
f) Name three great men of God who rejected gifts of
   unrighteous mammon.

g) What interests God more, our heart condition or size of money? Explain.

h) Summarize the message of this chapter in your own words.

Practical steps:

Examine your life and business. Are there ways you may be making money in an unrighteous way? Please repent.

CHAPTER SEVEN

SEX AND IMMORALITY

The body is not for fornication but for the Lord... flee fornication (1 Corinthians 6:13, 18).

But fornication, and all uncleanness, or covetousness, let it not be once named among you, as becometh saints (Ephesians 5:3).

Thought: Although men (and women) find great pleasure in sexual immorality, God has never hidden his hatred for it. That is why adulterers and adulteresses were stoned to death in the Old Testament.

An old but popular song says that "Sex makes the world go round." But the truth is that it makes the world go round and round until it is dumped into hell. God says to one of the churches in Revelation: *"Behold I will cast her into a bed, and them that commit adultery with her into great tribulation, except they repent of their deeds. And I will kill her children with death..."*

A true disciple of Christ must take heed not to get entangled with this old vice which has really gone epidemic, or rather pandemic, in these end-times. It is wisdom to beware of the real destructive effects of this sin which the Bible condemns from Genesis to Revelation.

Bible Warnings

In Old Testament times the penalty meted by God to fornicators and adulterers was death by stoning[103]. That says a lot about how God felt about the matter. And he has not changed his views on the gravity of the offence.

In the New Testament it is viewed as a defilement of the matrimonial bed[104], and Christ permitted it as a legitimate ground for divorce[105]. (This is only in cases where the aggrieved party is unwilling to forgive: but mercy rejoices against judgment.[106]) Fornication is listed among one of the signs for a reprobate mind[107], and fornicators and adulterers are listed among those who will go to hellfire (Revelation 21:8).

Scriptures affirm that, *"she hath cast down many wounded: yea, many strong men have been slain by her; her house is the way to hell, going down to the chambers of death"*[108]. Those who think they are strong should take heed, because she has cast down many strong men: David, a man after God's heart was one of them; Solomon, beloved of his God was another; Samson, the strongest man who ever lived, was among those cast down by her.

Sodom and Gomorrah were ruined by her, and others too numerous to mention. Ancient Israel went into captivity because of fornication[109].

Insidious Onset

We are warned to beware. Fornication starts insidiously in the mind, sometimes without observation. It then grows as a desire, and if it is allowed, and cherished, and is not rooted out early enough, it can become gradually entrenched. It may start with holding hands with members of the opposite sex longer than is meant.

It could start by watching sex movies on the television or Internet, and stirring up your emotions. If allowed, it will grow into a monster that sooner than later devours its owner. Flee fornication: that's what Joseph did, and retained his favour with God. His promotion to Prime Minister of Egypt came at the right season because he did not compromise with Potiphar's sexy wife. He refused to stay with her, or listen to her entreaties. Are you listening? *"Let not thine heart decline to her ways; go not astray in her paths"* (Proverbs 7:25). Your promotion will come when you have proven yourself.

Advice

- Avoid sex movies and pornographic materials.
- Avoid intoxicating drinks that alter your sense of judgment and discretion.
- Do not counsel the opposite sex alone, unless you keep the door wide open.
- Do not allow a compromising situation to arise.
- Your best friend and companion should be your spouse, or a member of same sex (not homosexual or lesbian!)
- Do not linger in holding hands with a man or woman who is not your spouse.
- Do not masturbate. It is defiling yourself, and it is provoking yourself.
- Dress properly, and do not expose your private regions.
- Watch what you look upon when you see a person of the opposite sex. Do not allow your eyes to become magnetized by their beauty.
- Admiration can linger into lust.

But every man is tempted, when he is drawn away of his own lust, and enticed. Then when lust hath conceived, it bringeth forth sin: and sin, when it is finished, bringeth forth death (James 1:15-16).

WORK BOOK

a) Why is God so seriously against fornication? What does he say about our bodies? (1 Corinthians 6:13, 18).

b) In Old Testament times what was the penalty for adultery? In the New Testament what is the end-result of it? What does the Bible prescribe to be done about church members who commit fornication or adultery?

c) Fornication and adultery *"hath cast down many wounded"* (Proverbs 7:26-27). Explain with illustrations.

d) Fornication starts insidiously in the heart. How can we deal with it before it turns into a giant that takes us captive? (Job 31:1-12; 1 Corinthians 6:18).

e) Name some great men of God in the Bible who fell into this sin. What should they have done?

f) What are the contemporary ways by which we are seduced to commit fornication? What should we do?

Practical steps:

Decide on some life principles you must adopt now in order to save yourself from this evil.

CHAPTER EIGHT

FOOD AND DRINK

When thou sittest to eat with a ruler, consider diligently what is before thee; and put a knife to thy throat if thou be a man given to appetite. Be not thou desirous of his dainties; for they are deceitful meat (Proverbs 23:1-3).

Wine is a mocker, strong drink is raging: and whosoever is deceived thereby is not wise (Proverbs 20:1).

Thought: Do not over-eat at night if you want to hear from God.

It would be unwise for any of us to disdain food and drink as possible reasons for falling from the faith. It has caused the downfall of many strong men. You ask how? It was with food that the world's first parents fell from grace. Adam and Eve disobeyed God's clear-cut instructions because Satan deceived them into believing that the fruit from the tree of knowledge of good and evil was exceptionally appetizing, and would give them the wisdom of the gods. So they ate it, contrary to God's command.

Satan's first arrow of temptation after Christ's 40-day fast was centred on food. Christ was hungry, and Satan encouraged him to use his power as the Son of God to turn stones unto bread, to assuage his hunger. This was a possible way for the

Lord to satisfy his hunger but the Lord did not consider it the wisest or the most expedient way. It would have been sin for him if he failed to restrain himself until proper food was available. Today there are many men who would do anything to satisfy their hunger for food, even unlawful things. Satan's will is for us to cast off all restraint because of food.

Esau lost his birth right because of his indiscretion when he was hungry. Esau, as first born of Isaac, would have occupied the position which Israel now occupies with God. It was lack of restraint with food that changed things forever. And we also run grave risks if we fail to restrain ourselves when we are hungry.

Noah and Lot were God's righteous men, but they got drunk, and their drunkenness brought disaster to their children[110].

And the book of Proverbs declares that *"the drunkard and the glutton shall come to poverty."* [111]

Apostle Paul warned the Roman Christians that drunkards shall not inherit the kingdom of God.[112]

And Paul further warns us, *"Destroy not him with thy meat, for whom Christ died".*[113] Friends, food is good, and drink is good: but God requires discretion and restraint from each one of us. Avoid gluttony because it will bring you to poverty in the things of God. You will not be able to hear clearly from God, and if you believe in taking a little alcohol "for your stomach's sake", one day you may get drunk, and sin against God.

There are many who could have prevailed with God and with men, but because of their love for food, they could not fast or pray as they should have done. There must be times and seasons when we should willingly give up food so that we can spend time with God in fasting and prayers. And at such times, even when we eat, we should do so with discretion so that we can still hear whatever God may be saying to us. If Jesus Christ, our Lord, fasted for 40 days and 40 nights, is it too much for any of us to also fast for four days, or for one week?

Thank God that today there are men of God who do forty days fasting (6am–6p.m), or more. Each of us should sometimes say "No" to food and drink, and even sex, and engage ourselves to seek the face of God. There are still issues that a believer might not be able to resolve without fasting and prayers. That is what the Lord said[114].

So, for the sake of food, destroy not the work that God wants to do in your life and in others. Do not let your appetite rule your sense of judgment.

WORK BOOK

a) What damages have food and unrestrained appetite done to the destinies of men? Name specific examples. What should they have done?
b) Name some dangers of alcohol consumption.
c) How often do you fast? Do you eat little things here and there when you are supposed to be fasting? What does that show?
d) Christ fasted for 40 days and nights before his ministry took off. What does that tell us? Who else did this?
e) Summarize the message of this chapter in your own words.

Practical steps:

Can you adopt one day per week for fasting and praying?

CHAPTER NINE

FAME, FORTUNE, POWER AND WORLDLY SUCCESS

Again the devil taketh him up into an exceedingly high mountain, and showeth him all the kingdoms of the world, and the glory of them. And saith unto him, All these things will I give thee, if thou wilt fall down and worship me (Matthew 4:8, 9).

Thought: Many, who are first here, will be the last there.

There is an innate desire in every one of us to be popular, well-respected, and even famous. No one wants to appear unsuccessful, or mediocre. No one wants to be looked upon as a weakling. We want to be powerful and popular. Many disciples will be tested with the opportunity for fame and power, and others who are in power already will be tested or tempted with the power they possess.

It was David's power that facilitated his adultery with Bathsheba. The same thing happened to Samson. They say **"Power corrupts, and absolute power corrupts absolutely."** So if you are in power already, or seeking for power, you will surely be tempted to compromise your faith in one way or another.

Satan will tempt us with opportunities to acquire power through unlawful means, even if we are not yet powerful. He will present unlawful quick-fix ways for us to rise to power. You must resist him, and refuse his offers. That is what Jesus, our pioneer, did. He rebuffed Satan's offers, and so must we if we want to be God's true disciples.

Not many people in today's world would readily say "No" to Satan's offer, because power feels so good, so sweet, so valuable, and so powerful! There are would-be Disciples of Christ who have been diverted into cults, secret societies, and occultism because powerful men have lured them into these groups with promises of power and fame. There are others who have diverted into churches with questionable or false doctrines, because of a promise of promotion.

There are ministers of the gospel who no longer preach about hell, or eternal judgment, or sin… all because they want more crowds of people in their churches. They love to become famous.

There are people, would-be disciples, who have bent backwards to accommodate some unscriptural doctrines (e.g. homosexuality, etc.) just so they can remain relevant with world opinion. And so on…

Attempts will surely be made at different times to get us to capitulate to pressure for power, promotion, and popularity but we should each be resolved not to give in to these pressures. We must be determined to stay on course with the unchanging Word of God. In due time God will vindicate all his word in our lives, and those that abide faithful to him and his word, will abide forever. If we remain faithful with his word, God's word will sustain us through to the end, in Jesus' name.

In conclusion, it is God's stated will for us to prosper[115], and to make us famous. He told Abraham, *"I will make your* name great"[116]. But we should seek this greatness only from God, not from men. The Lord Jesus said, *"I receive not honour from men"*[117]. This also should be our stand. Let us stop seeking for honour from men. Let us seek only the honour that comes from God. If we serve God acceptably with godly fear, in due time he will promote and exalt us, *"For promotion cometh neither from the east, nor from the west, nor from the south, but God is the judge; he putteth down one, and setteth up another"* (Psalm 75:6-7).

WORK BOOK

a) How did Satan tempt Christ with fame and success? How does he tempt us also?

b) Is it God's will for us to succeed in life, and become great? (Genesis 12:1-3).

c) Balaam the prophet was powerful in his day, and respected by kings. He knew the truth. But how and why did he succumb to the temptation for fame and riches? (Numbers 22. Note v. 16, 17). Why did God allow him to go? What was his final fate? (Numbers 31:8). What do we learn from this?

d) Christ said, *"I receive not honour of men"*. Discuss the implications for us. Do we or do we not receive?

e) In what ways do we seek and receive honour from men, and how has it affected the church?

f) Summarize the message of this chapter in your own words.

Practical steps:

Discuss this statement: *"God resisteth the proud, and giveth grace to the humble"* (1 Peter 5:5). Apply it to yourself.

CHAPTER TEN

ANGER, QUARRELS, BITTERNESS AND UNFORGIVENESS

Woe unto the world because of offences! For it must needs be that offences come, but woe to that man by whom the offence cometh! (Matthew 18:7).

Moreover if thy brother shall trespass against thee, go and tell him his fault between thee and him alone: if he shall hear thee, thou hast gained thy brother (Matthew 18:7, 15).

Simeon and Levi are brethren; instruments of cruelty are in their habitations. Cursed be their anger for it was fierce; and their wrath for it was cruel... (Genesis 49:5, 7).

Thought: Moses could not enter the Promised Land because of his "righteous anger."

Anger has done a lot of havoc in this world. Of course each person feels his or her own anger is justified, but I think we can learn a lot from Moses' anger; even though his anger was against the murmurings of the children of Israel, it made him to act unwisely, and he spoke unadvisedly with his lips[118], and because of this he was forbidden from entering the land of promise (Deuteronomy 3:23-27).

Anger has caused a lot of evil in our world: it has caused wars, countless murders, divorces, hatred, and every imaginable form of trouble. It is an evil that every disciple of Christ should by all means overcome; no matter how justified you may feel about your anger. Christ says that offences must come: this means that as long as we are in this world with fellow imperfect beings, we must be ready and waiting: someone must offend you sooner or later. In fact many people will offend you every day. Why? Because we are all sinners. Even you yourself will offend many people. You may easily forgive yourself, or justify your actions, but other people will prove you wrong.

Offences occur because we are sinners: we offend people because we are envious or jealous of them; or we acted selfishly without due consideration; or we acted out of greed and covetousness, or in ignorance. A disciple of Christ must take cognizance of human imperfections and make allowance for the faults of others. Even your much loved ones will offend you too: whether they be your spouse, or children, or parents, or colleagues, or relations. You must anticipate offences because Christ said "it must needs be that offences come".

Dealing with Offences

The usual worldly way to deal with offences is to react in anger, disillusionment, bitterness or quarrels. In many cases this will lead to fights, strife, bitterness, and un-forgiveness. There is a usual tendency to retaliate in one way or the other, and this will usually aggravate the enmity. If things are not settled by a mediator, the matter could progress further... and there have been murders and other atrocities committed because of some offences caused by some people against others. It is not news that there are many Christians today who are in enmity with one another, or with some other persons either in their home, offices, or church.

But for us Disciples of Christ, the teaching of the Lord must be obeyed in the matter of offences caused us by others. The golden rule is that we must forgive them. We must endeavour to forgive all offences that people commit against us. It is far better to forgive them, whether they repented or not.

The Lord Jesus said that if you bring your gift to the Lord, and at the altar you remember that your brother (or sister) has offended you, you should leave your gift there at the altar, and go first and reconcile with your brother (or, sister); then afterward you should come and offer your gift: otherwise your gifts and your prayers to God would not be acceptable to God (Matthew 5:23-26). Further (as mentioned earlier), we must be very careful of what we say in times of anger because the Lord teaches that one can come into eternal judgment for calling someone else *a fool.* And finally the Lord teaches also that if we do not forgive those who offend us "from our hearts[119]", then our own offences will not be forgiven by God. This is why the Lord calls us his sheep, and says we should be gentle as doves, and wise as serpents.

The Remedy

In conclusion, as heirs of God's kingdom, the Lord expects us to obey him completely in this seemingly difficult matter. God says we should love our enemies, and bless those that curse us, and rejoice when we are persecuted for his name's sake. We are not to render railing for railing or cursing for cursing, but contrariwise blessing. If our enemy hungers, we are to feed him; and if he thirsts we are to give him drink.

It is by these acts of love that we truly identify ourselves as children of God, and by these we will win many sinners back to God. We must emulate Christ our pioneer, who while on the cross still prayed for the offenders. This is how we can grow in Christlikeness, and become the ultimate disciples that God wants us to become. God's command to all who aspire to be like Christ is, *"Be not overcome of evil, but overcome evil with good"* (Romans 12:21). If there is cause for you to be angry, (and there will be many such causes) the Scriptures still admonish us, *"Be ye angry, and sin not: let not the sun go down upon your wrath; neither give place to the devil"* (Ephesians 4:26-27). Friends, let our love cover a multitude of sins[120].

WORK BOOK

a) It is accepted that "righteous anger" is good. But how did righteous anger work against Moses? (Numbers 20:1-13; Deuteronomy 3:23-26). What about Simeon and Levi?

b) Some people "get mad" with anger. Explain. Has it ever happened to you?

c) "Offences must come." Explain this statement of Jesus. How should we handle offences?

d) What is Christ's recommended way of dealing with those who offend us?

e) If you remember that your brother has "aught" against you, and you are at the altar to offer your gifts, what does the Lord say you should do? (Matthew 5:23-24). What does that teach us about God's will for us?

f) Christ said we should forgive our brothers *"from our hearts"* (Matthew 18:35). Is there someone you have not completely forgiven, from your heart?

g) Summarize the message of this chapter in your own words.

Practical steps:

Go and make peace, and completely forgive those that offended you; do it today, please.

CHAPTER ELEVEN

LIES AND FALSEHOOD

"Remove from me the way of lying" (Psalm 119:29)

"The devil... is a liar, and the father of it" (John 8:44)

Thought: When all has been said, we always still have to search for the truth: because only the truth will profit us.

All the evils that have befallen the world since creation to date have been due to a lie: they all resulted from the lie told by Satan the devil to Adam and Eve. That means that all the deaths, sorrows, sicknesses, evils, wars, earthquakes, and all other evils that have befallen humanity over many generations have been due to the negative and catastrophic power of lies and falsehood. And today men are still relentlessly engaging in telling lies and forging mischiefs with careless abandon. No wonder God's word declares that all liars will end up in hellfire. *"But the fearful and unbelieving... and all liars shall have their part in the lake which burneth with fire and brimstone: which is the second death"* (Revelations 21:8).

Lies prosper in the world because in many cases the lies are not discovered in time before the liars escape with their loot; and in some cases they are never discovered at all. Thus lies often provide an easy way of escape from penalties that we would have incurred. And lies help many unscrupulous people to quickly attain their personal selfish ambitions without stress, using unlawful short-cuts.

But God declares that lies originate from Satan, and that he (the devil) is the father of lies. Therefore those who tell lies are the children of the devil[121]. But we are of God, and God is the author of truth. Jesus said, "I am the way, the truth, and the life."

All around us are people who tell all kinds of lies, and seem to be getting away with them. They seem to be making great progress but in reality, as far as God is concerned, they are in the pits of hell.

People tell lies about their age, their motives, their bank accounts, credit worthiness, their parents, spouses, etc. They change figures, inflate invoices, lie about their expenses, hide information, cheat and lie about their activities and their roles. Sports celebrities take performance – enhancing drugs and lie about them. Husbands cheat on their wives, and wives on their husbands, and lie about it. Many people engage in examination malpractices and cover up on them. Others perpetuate fraud with office accounts, alter office records, or engage in other corrupt practices and feign innocence.

People forge lies, and "prosper", and many Christians find this quite tempting. We are enticed to tell small lies here and there, and gradually we graduate to bigger lies, and excuse ourselves on the pretext that everybody else is doing it. But we are not everybody else. We are God's special people, bought with the special price of the blood of the Son of God, not with corruptible silver and gold. It would be utter folly for us to step down from our steadfast commitment to the truth that is in Christ Jesus. The ultimate disciple cannot condescend to lying for cheap gain.

If we want to prevail with God (and with men), we who have chosen to live the Christ life must always stand on the truth, speak the truth, and nothing but the truth. God will prosper the truth in due course, and even where men try to kill the truth and bury it, sooner or later, truth will emerge again and prevail.

Truth may cause us hardship, but such hardship is only temporary. Eventually God will vindicate truth and promote it. But lies will bring men to doom and eternal destruction. There have been men who appeared to be on the very top of the ladder of success, whether in their profession, church, or business, but eventually the lie that they told and lived along the way dragged them down to the mud. Some of them ended up in prison, others in bankruptcy, and some even committed suicide. But even where lies are not uncovered in this world, they will be openly displayed in the life to come, on Judgment Day: and then it will be too late.

Therefore it is incumbent on every would-be disciple of Christ to be purged of every lie, whether big or small, because the book of Revelation in three separate scriptures emphasizes that *"No liar will inherit the kingdom of heaven."*[122].

- Truth will separate you from sinners
- Truth will sanctify you
- Truth justifies us
- Truth engenders godliness
- Truth endures to eternity
- Truth gives boldness
- Truth identifies us as God's children
- Truth will acquit us on Judgment Day
- Truth will distinguish you
- Truth will bring you honour and credibility

- Truth may bring you suffering and hardship sometimes but at last truth will vindicate you.

Therefore always stand on the truth, and never settle for any lie, whether big or small.

God bless you.

WORK BOOK

a) Why does God hate lying and deceit? Who is the originator (the father) of lies? Those who tell lies are the children of whom?
b) How can we be delivered from lying?
c) What does the Bible say is the fate of all liars? (Revelation 21:8; NIV).
d) Why do so many people tell lies? Do you know Christians who tell lies? Do you tell lies sometimes? Why?
e) Can truth be costly sometimes? But can we afford to live with lies? Can you pray effectively when you are living a life of lies?
f) Crucify the truth, bury it, deny it; yet truth will eventually resurrect. Discuss this. (Matthew 10:26).
g) Summarize the message of this chapter in your own words.

Practical steps:

If you have hurt people with lies, go and make amends today. Can you resolve today to live only by the truth?

CHAPTER TWELVE

WORLDLINESS (FRIENDSHIP WITH THE WORLD)

Ye adulterers and adulteresses, know ye not that the friendship of the world is enmity with God? Whosoever therefore will be a friend of the world is the enemy of God (James 4:4).

Love not the world, neither the things that are in the world. If any man love the world, the love of the Father is not in him (1 John 2:15).

…Demas hath forsaken me, having loved this present world (2 Timothy 4:10).

Thought: It would be great folly for any of us to underrate the attractive pull of the fading glory of this present world.

Christ was tempted with earthly glory when the devil took him to a high mountain and showed him *"all the kingdoms of the world, and the glory of them"*[123]. But the Lord declined his offers.

Today many men have willingly embraced Satan's offers, and even many Christians are of two opinions when they behold the "glory", the riches, the honours, the fame, the fashions, and the pleasures that the world has to offer.

This world is filled with all kinds of programmes, projects, events, celebrations, and activities that can fully occupy anyone without giving any allowance for God. Television alone with all its news, movies, sports, and other attractions can fully engage you twenty-four hours a day. What about the internet, the social media, Facebook, twitter, video-games, communications, and others?

What about social events: dating, marriage, birthdays, burials, parties, club events, sporting events, night clubs, boyfriends, girlfriends, premarital and extramarital relationships, drinking, orgies, etc.?

What about business meetings, deadlines, innovations, and buying and selling, and the relentless drive for making more money?

The world is a very busy place indeed, and virtually everyone is seriously engaged in the pursuit of one goal or another. And at the end of the day people have some accomplishment to flaunt: more houses bought, or more money in the bank, or more fame, or more laurels, or stories about some pleasure-trip or holidays that is "out of this world", new friendships struck, new dates, new joys, etc.

It all sounds so exciting, so attractive. And we are all tempted to join, to celebrate with the world. In fact the world would wonder why you are not joining in the celebration and in the activities. Many people would think that you are losing out on life, and they will pity you for being so strict on yourself! Others will think you are a crank, and many will sneer at your religion. They will wonder if something has gone wrong with you. Jesus said that the world will say to you, *"We have piped unto you, and ye have not danced; we have mourned unto you, and ye have not lamented"*[124].

The unfortunate thing is that many Christians, in order to "prove" to the world that they are not better than themselves, often join in these worldly activities and festivities. Some Christians patronize beer parlours, and even brothels. Some sing and dance to worldly music that does not glorify Christ at all.

Some believers go on business trips and have affairs with business associates or their secretaries, or bosses. Many Christians have no qualms about making shady business deals, and do not care much how they make their money. Some give bribes, and take bribes, and then come to testify in church about their business breakthrough. Many Christians go to night clubs, and some watch any kind of movies, not caring about the immoral sex content, filling their hearts with lust and adultery. Today many Christians divorce their spouses just like the unbelievers. Abortion is common even among the saints today. Some are even homosexuals and lesbians.

Many Christians freely admit to premarital and extramarital sex, and other infidelities. Many also tell lies, just like the unbelievers. And we gossip about other people, and criticize freely. Many Christians hardly pray any more, or even give any serious attention to Bible studies. Even going to church or fellowship is a hurdle for some, as they claim they hear their sermons on TV.

Sometimes the relationships between the saints and the sinners are so close that you may no longer be able to tell who the saint is, or who the sinner is. That is what the Bible calls a mixed multitude, and it is seen today in many congregations. Christ had prophesied that it would be so. But he said,

> *Let them grow together until the harvest; and in the time
> of harvest I will say to the reapers, Gather ye together
> first the tares, and bind them in bundles to burn them;
> but gather the wheat into my barn* (Matthew 13:30).

In the light of these things, what should a Christian who aspires to make heaven do?

Separate Yourself!

God has a clear instruction and command to every one of his children who aspires to walk in the steps of Christ. He says we must separate ourselves; we must disengage ourselves from this closeness with the world. It does not matter whether the worldly people are, or were, our closest brothers, or friends or colleagues.

We must put a safe distance between us and them in our dealings, lest they draw us back into the world. Yes, we are to love them, and we are to witness to them in a bid to recover them for Christ, but we must do this with the wisdom of God, and from a safe distance for the sake of our souls. God hates worldliness. Whosoever will be a friend of the world is the enemy of God. Take advice, and listen to what God has said.

> *Wherefore come out from among them, and be ye
> separate, saith the Lord, and touch not the unclean
> thing; and I will receive you, and will be a Father unto
> you, and ye shall be my sons and daughters, saith the
> Lord Almighty* (2 Corinthians 6:17-18).

WORK BOOK

a) What does God say about friendship with the world? (James 4:4; 1 John 2:15). Can you explain "friendship with the world"?

b) What would you say was the sin of Lot's wife? Why did she look back? Her other daughters and their husbands were not rescued by the angels. Why? Do you think Lot's wife may have influenced them to become worldly?

c) Are there any attractive pulls in the world for today's Christians?

d) What is worldliness? Describe some worldliness we see in the church and in many Christians today.

e) Give suggestions on how church leaders and Christians generally can reduce worldliness in today's church. What about discipline?

f) When God says, *"Separate yourselves from among them"* (2 Corinthians 6:17-18), what does he mean?

Practical steps:

Be not unequally yoked together with unbelievers (2 Corinthians 6:14). Define ways in which this applies to you, and state what you must do to disengage.

SCRIPTURAL REFERENCES

These are the Scriptural References in:

Chapter 1
1. Acts 4:13
2. 2 Timothy 1:14
3. Hebrews 5:12

Chapter 2
4. 1 Peter 1:2
5. Ephesians 4:22
6. Proverbs 21:30
7. 1 John 3:2
8. 1 Peter 2:21
9. Philippians 3:10
10. Philippians 3:14

Chapter 3
11. Ephesians 4:11-13
12. Matthew 11:29-30
13. 2 Peter 3:18
14. 1 John 2:12-14
15. 2 Peter 3:18
16. 2 Timothy 3:5
17. Matthew 25:1-12
18. 1 John 4:17
19. Acts 2:22
20. 1 John 4:17
21. Revelation 21:27

Chapter 4

22. 1 Timothy 6:9-10
23. Colossians 3:3
24. Hebrews 11:10
25. 2 Peter 3:14
26. John 14:10
27. John 14:10
28. Romans 8:13
29. Colossians 1:27; 2 Corinthians 3:17
30. John 15:5
31. Luke 11:13
32. 2 Corinthians 6:16
33. Acts 19:1-6
34. Mark 1:9-10
35. Psalm 2:11
36. Romans 5:17, 4:22-25
37. Matthew 5:48
38. Philippians 2:12
39. Philippians 2:13
40. 2 Corinthians 10:3-5
41. Matthew 12:37
42. James 3:2
43. John 13:4-5
44. John 11:40
45. Matthew 15:28, 8:10-11
46. Hebrews 5:7
47. Matthew 15:9; Mark 7:7
48. Revelation 12:11
49. 1 John 2:15; James 4:4
50. Luke 16:19-31 (NKJV)
51. James 1:27
52. Matthew 5:44

53. Romans 10:1

54. Matthew 12:36

55. Deuteronomy 3:25-27

56. 2 Chronicles 16:9

57. Mark 6:31

58. Ecclessiastes11:4

59. 2 Corinthians 5:19

60. 2 Corinthians 6:16

61. Jeremiah 1:17

62. John 7:26; Acts 4:13; Mark 10:32

63. Acts 4:13, 29, 31, 14:3

64. 2 Corinthians 10:1, 2; 1 Thessalonians 2:2; Acts 9:27, 19:8; Ephesians 6:19

65. Acts 13:46

66. Acts 18:26

67. Proverbs 28:1

68. John 14:21, 23

69. Psalm 119:11

70. Matt 17:21

71. Daniel 6:1-28

72. 1 Samuel 2:30

73. Proverbs 8:17

74. 2 Chronicles 19:7, 9

75. Job 28:28

76. Psalm 19:7-9

77. Proverbs 8:13

78. Proverbs 10:27

79. Proverbs 14:27

80. Ecclesiastes 12:13

81. Matthew 10:28

82. Revelation 19:5

83. Revelation 14:7

Chapter 8

110. Genesis 9:20-27, 19:30-38
111. Proverbs 23:21
112. 1 Corinthians 6:10
113. Romans 14:15
114. Matthew 17:21

Chapter 9

115. 3 John 2
116. Genesis 12:2
117. John 5:41

Chapter 10

118. Numbers 20:2-13; Psalm 103:32, 33
119. Matthew 18:35
120. 1 Peter 4:8

Chapter 11

121. 1 John 3:10
122. Revelation 21:8, 21:27, 22:15

Chapter 12

123. Matthew 4:8
124. Matthew 11:17

STEPS TO SALVATION

Acknowledge - *"...Be merciful unto me a sinner"* (Luke 8:13).

Confess - *"If we confess our sin, He is faithful and just to forgive us our sins and cleanse us from all unrighteousness"* (1 John 1:9).

Repent - *"Except ye repent ye shall all likewise perish"* (Luke 13:3). *"Repent ye therefore, and be converted that your sins may be blotted out"* (Acts 3:19).

Forsake - *"Let the wicked forsake his ways, and the unrighteous man his thoughts, and let him return unto the Lord, and He will have mercy upon him, and to our God, for He will abundantly pardon"* (Isaiah 55:7).

Believe - *"He that believeth and is baptized shall be saved: but he that believeth not shall be damned"* (Mark 16:16).

Receive - *"He came unto his own and his own received him not. But as many as received Him, to them gave he power to become the sons of God, even to them that believed on his name"* (John 1:11-12).

Abide - *"Abide in me, and I in you. As the branch cannot bear fruit of itself, except it abide in the vine; no more can ye, except ye abide in me"* (John 15:4).

Apart from your personal use, "The Ultimate Disciple" may also be used for Discipleship training in Churches, Fellowships, Groups and Families. If you desire more information on how to use this Book to set up Discipleship groups, please contact the Author.

Dr. Bennett U. Okafor
P. O. Box 2330, Port Harcourt,
Rivers State, Nigeria.
E-mail: necoportcity@yahoo.com
Phone: (+234) 817 538 1275; (+234) 803 312 3024.
Website: www.neconetwork.org

ABOUT THE AUTHOR

Dr. Bennett U. Okafor and his wife, Laide, are Spirit-filled believers. They are proprietors and medical directors of a private Christian Hospital in Port Harcourt, Rivers State, Nigeria. They are blessed with four children.

Dr. Okafor is an ordained priest of the Anglican Communion and is currently serving at St. Paul's Cathedral, Port Harcourt. He is also the International Coordinator of National Evangelism Christian Outreach (NECO) Inc., and has outreach and Church planting ministries in eight French-speaking African nations. He has a passion for preaching righteousness and mobilizing church-congregations for greater evangelism exploits.